Vampires and V

Dudley Wright

Alpha Editions

This edition published in 2024

ISBN : 9789362923134

Design and Setting By
Alpha Editions
www.alphaedis.com
Email - info@alphaedis.com

Contents

PREFACE

The awakened interest in supernormal phenomena which has taken place in recent years has included in its wake the absorbing subject of Vampirism. Yet there has not been any collection published of vampire stories which are common to all the five continents of the globe. The subject of vampirism is regarded more seriously to-day than it was even a decade since, and an attempt has been made in this volume to supply as far as possible all the instances which could be collected from the various countries. How far a certain amount of scientific truth may underlie even what may be regarded as the most extravagant stories must necessarily be, for the present, at any rate, an open question; but he would indeed be a bold man who would permit[v] his scepticism as to the objective existence of vampires in the past or the possibility of vampirism in the future to extend to a categorical denial. If this collection of stories helps, even in a slight degree, to the elucidation of the problem, the book will not have been written in vain.

DUDLEY WRIGHT.

AUTHORS' CLUB, 2 WHITEHALL COURT, S.W.,
1st September, 1914.

CHAPTER I
INTRODUCTORY

What is a vampire? The definition given in Webster's *International Dictionary* is: "A blood-sucking ghost or re-animated body of a dead person; a soul or re-animated body of a dead person believed to come from the grave and wander about by night sucking the blood of persons asleep, causing their death."

Whitney's *Century Dictionary* says that a vampire is: "A kind of spectral body which, according to a superstition existing among the Slavic and other races on the Lower Danube, leaves the grave during the night and maintains a semblance of life by sucking the warm blood of living men and women while they are asleep. Dead wizards, werwolves, heretics, and other outcasts become vampires, as do also the illegitimate offspring of parents themselves illegitimate, and anyone killed by a vampire."

According to the *Encyclopædia Britannica*: "The persons who turn vampires are generally wizards, suicides, and those who come to a violent end or have been cursed by their parents or by the Church. But anyone may become a vampire if an animal (especially a cat) leaps over the corpse or a bird flies over it."

Among the specialists, the writers upon vampire lore and legend, two definitions may be quoted:—Hurst, who says that: "A vampyr is a dead body which continues to live in the grave; which it leaves, however, by night, for the purpose of sucking the blood of the living, whereby it is nourished and preserved in good condition, instead of becoming decomposed like other dead bodies"; and Scoffern, who wrote: "The best definition I can give of a vampire is a living mischievous and murderous dead body. A living dead body! The words are idle, contradictory, incomprehensible, but so are vampires."

"Vampires," says the learned Zopfius, "come out of their graves in the night time, rush upon people sleeping in their beds, suck out all their blood and destroy them. They attack men, women, and children, sparing neither age nor sex. Those who are under the malignity of their influence complain of suffocation and a total deficiency of spirits, after which they soon expire. Some of them being asked at the point of death what is the matter with them, their answer is that such persons lately dead rise to torment them."

Not all vampires, however, are, or were, suckers of blood. Some, according to the records, despatched their victims by inflicting upon them contagious diseases, or strangling them without drawing blood, or causing their speedy or retarded death by various other means.

Messrs Skeat and Blagden, in *Pagan Races of the Malay Peninsula* (vol. i. p. 473), state that "a vampire, according to the view of Sakai of Perak, is not a demon—even though it is incidentally so-called—but a being of flesh and blood," and support this view by the statement that the vampire cannot pass through walls and hedges.

The word *vampire* (Dutch, *vampyr*; Polish, *wampior* or *upior*; Slownik, *upir*; Ukraine, *upeer*) is held by Skeat to be derived from the Servian *wampira*. The Russians, Morlacchians, inhabitants of Montenegro, Bohemians, Servians, Arnauts, both of Hydra and Albania, know the vampire under the name of *wukodalak*, *vurkulaka*, or *vrykolaka*, a word which means "wolf-fairy," and is thought by some to be derived from the Greek. In Crete, where Slavonic influence has not been felt, the vampire is known by the name of *katakhaná*. Vampire lore is, in general, confined to stories of resuscitated corpses of male human beings, though amongst the Malays a *penangglan*, or vampire, is a living witch, who can be killed if she can be caught in the act of witchery. She is especially feared in houses where a birth has taken place, and it is the custom to hang up a bunch of thistle in order to catch her. She is said to keep vinegar at home to aid her in re-entering her own body. In the Malay Peninsula, parts of Polynesia and the neighbouring districts, the vampire is conceived as a head with entrails attached, which comes forth to suck the blood of living human beings. In Transylvania, the belief prevails that every person killed by a *nosferatu* (vampire) becomes in turn a vampire, and will continue to suck the blood of other innocent people until the evil spirit has been exorcised, either by opening the grave of the suspected person and driving a stake through the corpse, or firing a pistol-shot into the coffin. In very obstinate cases it is further recommended to cut off the head, fill the mouth with garlic, and then replace the head in its proper place in the coffin; or else to extract the heart and burn it, and strew the ashes over the grave.

The *murony* of the Wallachians not only sucks blood, but also possesses the power of assuming a variety of shapes, as, for instance, those of a cat, dog, flea, or spider; in consequence of which the ordinary evidence of death caused by the attack of a vampire, viz. the mark of a bite in the back of the neck, is not considered indispensable. The Wallachians have a very great fear of sudden death, greater perhaps than any other people, for they attribute sudden death to the attack of a vampire, and believe that anyone destroyed by a vampire must become a vampire, and that no power can save him from this fate. A similar belief obtains in Northern Albania, where it is also held that a wandering spirit has power to enter the body of any individual guilty of undetected crime, and that such obsession forms part of his punishment.

Some writers have ascribed the origin of the belief in vampires to Greek Christianity, but there are traces of the superstition and belief at a considerably earlier date than this. In the opinion of the anthropologist Tylor, "the shortest way of treating the belief is to refer it directly to the principles of savage animism. We shall see that most of its details fall into their places at once, and that vampires are not mere creations of groundless fancy, but causes conceived in spiritual form to account for specific facts of wasting disease." It is more than probable that the practice of offering up living animals as sacrifices to satisfy the thirst of departed human beings, combined with the ideas of the Platonist and the teachings of the learned Jew, Isaac Arbanel, who maintained that before the soul can be loosed from the fetters of the flesh it must lie some months with it in the grave, may have influenced the belief and assisted its development. Vampirism found a place in Babylonian belief and in the folk-lore and traditions of many countries of the Near East. The belief was quite common in Arabia, although there is no trace of it there in pre-Christian times. The earliest references to vampires are found in Chaldean and Assyrian tablets. Later, the pagan Romans gave their adherence to the belief that the dead bodies of certain people could be allured from their graves by sorcerers, unless the bodies had actually undergone decomposition, and that the only means of effectually preventing such "resurrections" was by cremating the remains. In Grecian lore there are many wonderful stories of the dead rising from their graves and feasting upon the blood of the young and beautiful. From Greece and Rome the superstition spread throughout Austria, Hungary, Lorraine, Poland, Roumania, Iceland, and even to the British Isles, reaching its height in the period from 1723 to 1735, when a vampire fever or epidemic broke out in the south-east of Europe, particularly in Hungary and Servia. The belief in vampires even spread to Africa, where the Kaffirs held that bad men alone live a second time and try to kill the living by night. According to a local superstition of the Lesbians, the unquiet ghost of the Virgin Gello used to haunt their island, and was supposed to cause the deaths of young children.

Various devices have been resorted to in different countries at the time of burial, in the belief that the dead could thus be prevented from returning to earth-life. In some instances, *e.g.* among the Wallachians, a long nail was driven through the skull of the corpse, and the thorny stem of a wild rose-bush laid upon the body, in order that its shroud might become entangled with it, should it attempt to rise. The Kroats and Slavonians burned the straw upon which the suspected body lay. They then locked up all the cats and dogs, for if these animals stepped over the corpse it would assuredly return as a vampire and suck the blood of the village folk. Many held that to drive a white thorn stake through the dead body rendered the vampire harmless, and the peasants of Bukowina still retain the practice of driving an ash stake through the breasts of suicides and supposed vampires—a practice common in England, so far as suicides were concerned, until 1823, when there was passed "An Act to alter and amend the law relating to the interment of the remains of any person found *felo de se*," in which it was enacted that the coroner or other officer "shall give directions for the private interment of the remains of such person *felo de se* without any stake being driven through the body of such person." It was also ordained that the burial was only to take place between nine and twelve o'clock at night.

The driving of a stake through the body does not seem to have had always the desired effect. De Schartz, in his *Magia Postuma*, published at Olmutz in 1706, tells of a shepherd in the village of Blow, near Kadam, in Bohemia, who made several appearances after his death and called certain persons, who never failed to die within eight days of such call. The peasants of Blow took up the body and fixed it to the ground by means of a stake driven through the corpse. The man, when in that condition, told them that they were very good to give him a stick with which he could defend himself against the dogs which worried him. Notwithstanding the stake, he got up again that same night, alarmed many people, and, presumably out of revenge, strangled more people in that one night than he had ever done on a single occasion before. It was decided to hand over his body to the public executioner, who was ordered to see that the remains were burned outside the village. When the executioner and his assistants attempted to move the corpse for that purpose, it howled like a madman, and moved its feet and hands as though it were alive. They then pierced the body through with stakes, but he again uttered loud cries and a great quantity of bright vermilion blood flowed from him. The cremation, however, put an end to the apparition and haunting of the spectre. De Schartz says that the only remedy for these apparitions is to cut off the heads and burn the bodies of those who come back to haunt their former abodes. It was, however, customary to hold a public inquiry and examination of witnesses before proceeding to the burning of a body, and if, upon examination of the body, it was found that the corpse had begun to decompose, that the limbs were not supple and mobile, and the blood not fluidic, then burning was not commanded. Even in the case of suspected persons an interval of six to seven weeks was always allowed to lapse before the grave was opened in order to ascertain whether the flesh had decayed and the limbs lost their suppleness and mobility. A Strigon or Indian vampire, who was transfixed with a sharp thorn cudgel, near Larbach, in 1672, pulled it out of his body and flung it back contemptuously.

Bartholin, in *de Causa contemptûs mortis*, tells the story of a man, named Harpye, who ordered his wife to bury him exactly at the kitchen door, in order that he might see what went on in the house. The woman executed her commission, and soon after his death he appeared to several people in the neighbourhood, killed people while they were engaged in their occupations, and played so many mischievous pranks that the inhabitants began to move away from the village. At last a man named Olaus Pa took courage and ran at the spectre with a lance, which he drove into the apparition. The spectre instantly vanished, taking the spear with it. Next morning Olaus had the grave of Harpye opened, when he found the lance in the dead body, which had not become corrupted. The corpse was then taken from the grave, burned, and the ashes thrown into the sea, and the spectre did not afterwards trouble the inhabitants.

To cross the arms of the corpse, or to place a cross or crucifix upon the grave, or to bury a suspected corpse at the junction of four cross-roads, was, in some parts, regarded as an efficacious preventive of vampirism. It will be remembered that it was at one time the practice in England to bury suicides at the four cross-roads. If a vampire should make its appearance, it could be prevented from ever appearing again by forcing it to take the oath not to do so, if the words "by my winding-sheet" were incorporated in the oath.

One charm employed by the Wallachians to prevent a person becoming a vampire was to rub the body in certain parts with the lard of a pig killed on St Ignatius's Day.

In Poland and Russia, vampires make their appearance from noon to midnight instead of between nightfall and dawn, the rule that generally prevails. They come and suck the blood of living men and animals in such abundance that sometimes it flows from them at the nose and ears, and occasionally in such profusion that the corpse swims in the blood thus oozing from it as it lies in the coffin. One may become immune from the attacks of vampires by mixing this blood with flour and making bread from the mixture, a portion of which must be eaten; otherwise the charm will not work. The Californians held that the mere breaking of the spine of the corpse was sufficient to prevent its return as a vampire. Sometimes heavy stones were piled on the grave to keep the ghost within, a practice to which Frazer traces the origin of funeral cairns and tombstones. Two resolutions of the Sorbonne, passed between 1700 and 1710, prohibited the cutting off of the heads and the maiming of the bodies of persons supposed to be vampires.

In the German folk-tale known as *Faithful John*, the statue said to the king: "If you, with your own hand, cut off the heads of both your children and sprinkle me with their blood, I shall be brought to life again." According to primitive ideas, blood is life, and to receive blood is to receive life: the soul of the dead wants to live, and, consequently, loves blood. The shades in Hades are eager to drink the blood of Odysseus's sacrifice, that their life may be renewed for a time. It is of the greatest importance that the soul should get what it desires, as, if not satisfied, it might come and attack the living. It is possible that the bodily mutilations which to this day accompany funerals among some peoples have their origin in the belief that the departed spirit is refreshed by the blood thus spilt. The Samoans called it an "offering of blood" for the dead when the mourners beat their heads till the blood ran.

The Australian native sorcerers are said to acquire their magical influence by eating human flesh, but this is done once only in a lifetime. According to Nider's *Formicarius*, part of the ceremony of initiation into wizardry and witchcraft consisted in drinking in a church, before the commencement of Mass, from a flask filled with blood taken from the corpses of murdered infants.

The methods employed for the detection of vampires have varied according to the countries in which the belief in their existence was maintained. In some places it was held that, if there were discovered in a grave two or three or more holes about the size of a man's finger, it would almost certainly follow that a body with all the marks of vampirism would be discovered within the grave. The Wallachians employed a rather elaborate method of divination. They were in the habit of choosing a boy young enough to make it certain that he was innocent of any impurity. He was then placed on an absolutely black and unmutilated horse which had never stumbled. The horse was then made to ride about the cemetery and pass over all the graves. If the horse refused to pass over any grave, even in spite of repeated blows, that grave was believed to shelter a vampire. Their records state that when such a grave was opened it was generally found to contain a corpse as fat and handsome as that of a full-blooded man quietly sleeping. The finest vermilion blood would flow from the throat when cut, and this was held to be the blood he had sucked from the veins of living people. It is said that the attacks of the vampire generally ceased on this being done.

In the town of Perlepe, between Monastru and Kiuprili, there existed the extraordinary phenomenon of a number of families who were regarded as being the offspring of *vrykolakas*, and as possessing the power of laying the wandering spirits to which they were related. They are said to have kept their art very dark and to have practised it in secret, but their fame was so widely spread that persons in need of such deliverance were accustomed to send for them from other cities. In ordinary life and intercourse they were avoided by all the inhabitants.

Although some writers have contended that no vampire has yet been caught in the act of vampirism, and that, as no museum of natural history has secured a specimen, the whole of the stories concerning vampires may be regarded as mythical, others have held firmly to a belief in their existence and inimical power. Dr Pierart, in *La Revue Spiritualiste* (vol. iv. p. 104), wrote: "After a crowd of facts of vampirism so often proved, shall we say that there are no more to be had, and that these never had a foundation? Nothing comes of nothing. Every belief, every custom, springs from facts and causes which give it birth. If one had never seen appear in the bosom of their families, in various countries, beings clothed in the appearance of departed ones known to them, sucking the blood of one or more persons, and if the deaths of the victims had not followed after such apparitions, the disinterment of corpses would not have taken place, and there would never have been the attestation of the otherwise incredible fact of persons buried for several years being found with the body soft and flexible, the eyes wide open, the complexion rosy, the mouth and nose full of blood, and the blood flowing fully when the body was struck or wounded or the head cut off."

Bishop d'Avranches Huet wrote: "I will not examine whether the facts of vampirism, which are constantly being reported, are true, or the fruit of a popular error; but it is beyond doubt that they are testified to by so many able and trustworthy authors, and by so many *eye-witnesses*, that no one ought to decide the question without a good deal of caution."

Dr Pierart gave the following explanation of their existence: "Poor, dead cataleptics, buried as if really dead in cold and dry spots where morbid causes are incapable of effecting the destruction of their bodies, the astral spirit, enveloping itself with a fluidic ethereal body, is prompted to quit the precincts of its tomb and to exercise on living bodies acts peculiar to physical life, especially that of nutrition, the result of which, by a mysterious link between soul and body which spiritualistic science will some day explain, is forwarded to the material body lying still within its tomb, and the latter is thus helped to perpetuate its vital existence."

Apart from the spectre vampire there is, of course, the vampire bat in the world of natural history, which is said to suck blood from a sleeping person, insinuating its tongue into a vein, but without inflicting pain. Captain Steadman, during his expedition to Surinam, awoke early one morning and was alarmed to find his hammock steeped almost through and himself weltering in blood, although he was without pain. It was discovered that he had been bitten by a vampire bat. Pennant says that in some parts of America they destroyed all the cattle introduced by the missionaries.

CHAPTER II
EXCOMMUNICATION AND ITS POWER

The Greek Church at one time taught that the bodies of persons upon whom the ban of excommunication had been passed did not undergo decomposition after death until such sentence had been revoked by the pronouncement of absolution over the remains, and that, while the bodies remained in this uncorrupted condition, the spirits of the individuals wandered up and down the earth seeking sustenance from the blood of the living. The non-corruption of a body, however, was also held to be one of the proofs of sanctity; but, in this case, the body preserved its natural colour and gave an agreeable odour, whereas the bodies of the excommunicated generally turned black, swelled out like a drum, and emitted an offensive smell. Very frequently, however, when the graves of suspected vampires were opened, the faces were found to be of ruddy complexion and the veins distended with blood, which, when opened with a lancet, yielded a supply of blood as plentiful, fresh, and free as that found in the veins of young and healthy living human beings. For many centuries in the history of Greek Christianity there was scarcely a village that had not its own local vampire stories which were related by the inhabitants and vouched for by them as having either occurred within their own knowledge or been related to them by their parents or relatives as having come within their personal observation or been verified by them.

The bodies of murderers and suicides were also held to be exempt from the law of dissolution of the mortal remains until the Church granted release from the curse entailed upon them by such act. The priests, by this assumption of power over the body as well as over the soul, made profitable use of this superstitious belief by preying upon the fears and credulity of the living. They also included in this ecclesiastical law of exemption from corruption after death those who in their lives had been guilty of heinous sins, those who had tampered with the magic arts, and all who had been cursed during life by their parents. These were all said to become vampires. This belief spread to other branches of the Christian Church, and the story is related that St Libentius, Archbishop of Bremen, who died 4th January 1013, once excommunicated a gang of pirates, one of whom died shortly afterwards and was buried in Norway. Seventy years afterwards his body was found quite entire and uncorrupted, nor did it fall to ashes until it had received absolution from the Bishop Alvareda.

Leo Allatius, a Roman Catholic, describes a corpse which he found in an undecomposed condition. He implies that the Greeks connected the circumstance with the power invested in them by the text: "Whatsoever thou shalt bind on earth shall be bound in heaven," and by which they hold that the soul is excluded from all hope of participation in future bliss so long as the body remains undecomposed. Poqueville, another writer, also states that whenever a bishop or priest excommunicated a person he added to the general sentence of excommunication the words: "After death, let not thy body have power to dissolve."

A manuscript was discovered many years ago in the Church of St Sophia at Thessalonica, which is an interesting commentary upon the power claimed by the Church over excommunicated bodies. The manuscript states that:

(1) Whoever has been laid under any curse or received any injunction from his deceased parents that he has not fulfilled, after his death the forepart of his body remains entire;

(2) Whoever has been the object of any anathema appears yellow after death, and the fingers are shrivelled;

(3) Whoever appears white has been excommunicated by the divine laws;

(4) Whoever appears black has been excommunicated by a bishop.

It was held possible to discover, by means of these signs, the crime for which, as well as the person on whom, the judgment had been pronounced. One horrible result of this ghastly superstition was the custom which was at one time prevalent among the Greeks of Salonica, as well as the Bulgarians in the centre of European Turkey, and other nations, of disinterring indiscriminately the bodies of the dead after they had been buried for twelve months, in order to ascertain from the condition of the remains whether the souls were in heaven or hell, or perambulating the neighbourhood as vampires.

This assumed ecclesiastical power acted occasionally, however, injuriously on the clergy themselves. There is on record one instance where a priest was killed in revenge for the death of a man whose illness was attributed to the sentence of excommunication that had been passed upon him. On another occasion a bishop of some diocese in Morea was robbed by a band of brigands as he was passing through a portion of the Maniate territory. When the deed was done the mountaineers bethought themselves that the bishop would, in all probability, excommunicate them as soon as he reached a place of safety. They saw no means of averting this, to them, dreadful calamity, except by the committal of a further and more heinous crime; and so they set out in pursuit of the unfortunate bishop, whom they eventually overtook and murdered.

Many years ago a Greek of Keramia complained to the Pasha of Khania that the papás of his village had excommunicated him and so been the indirect cause of his having been bewitched. The Pasha sent for the priest, threw him into prison, and only released him upon payment of a fine of 300 piastres.

During a local war a native of Theriso was taken ill: the cry went up: "It is an aphorismos." The papás was accused, reviled, and threatened with murder unless the curse was removed; but the man continued to get worse, and eventually died. So firm was the belief of everyone in the neighbourhood that the ban had caused the man's death that some of his companions regarded it as a duty to avenge his fate, and, in consequence, they sought out the priest and shot him.

At the beginning of the nineteenth century the Metropolitan of Larissa was informed that a papás had disinterred two bodies and thrown them into the Haliæmon on pretence of their being vrukólakas. Upon being summoned before the bishop the priest admitted the truth of the accusation, and justified his act by saying that a report had been current that a large animal, accompanied with flames, had been seen to issue from the grave in which these two bodies had been buried. The bishop fined the priest 250 piastres, and sent a proclamation throughout the diocese that, in future, similar offences would be punished with double that fine and be accompanied with loss of position.

Martin Crusius tells the following curious story. There were about the court of Mahomet II. a number of men learned in Greek and Arabic literature, who had investigated a variety of points connected with the Christian faith. They informed the Sultan that the bodies of persons excommunicated by the Greek clergy did not decompose, and when he inquired whether the effect of absolution was to dissolve them, he was answered in the affirmative. Upon this, he sent orders to Maximus, the Patriarch of that period, to produce a case by which the truth of the statement might be tested. The Patriarch convened his clergy in great trepidation, and after long deliberation they ascertained that a woman had been excommunicated by the previous Patriarch for the commission of grievous sins. They ascertained the whereabouts of her grave, and when they had opened it they found that the corpse was entire, but swollen out like a drum. When the news of this reached the Sultan, he despatched some of his officers to possess themselves of the body, which they did, and deposited it in a safe place. On an appointed day the liturgy was said over it and the Patriarch recited the absolution in the presence of the officials. As this was being done—wonderful to relate!—the bones were heard to rattle as they fell apart in the coffin, and at the same time, the narrator adds, the woman's soul was also freed from the punishment to which it had been condemned. The courtiers at once ran and informed the Sultan, who was astonished at the miracle, and exclaimed: "Of a surety the Christian religion is true." Calmet also relates this story, and adds that the body was found to be entirely black and much swollen; that it was placed in a chest under the Emperor's seal, which chest was not opened until three days after the absolution had been pronounced, when the body was seen to be reduced to ashes.

During the long war between the Christians and Mohammedans in the island of Crete, it became a matter of astonishment that ravages caused by vampires were no longer the subject of conversation. "How can it be, when the number of deaths is so great, that none of those that die become katakhanás?" was the question asked, to be met with the answer: "No one ever becomes a katakhaná if he dies in time of war."

Leo Allatius also relates that he was told by Athanasius, Metropolitan of Imbros, that, on one occasion, being earnestly entreated to pronounce the absolution over a number of corpses that had long remained undecomposed, he consented to do so, and before the recitation was concluded they all fell away into ashes.

Rycaut relates a similar occurrence, to which he appends the following remark: "This story I should not have judged worth relating, but that I heard it from the mouth of a grave person who says that his own eyes were witnesses thereof."

The Hydhræans (or Hydhrioks) say there used to be a great number of vampires in Hydhra, and that their present freedom is to be attributed solely to the exertions of their bishop, who banished them all to Santoréhe, where, on the desert isle, they now exist in great numbers, wandering about, rolling stones down the slope towards the sea, "as may be heard by anyone who passes near, in a kaík, during the night."

At the second Council of Limoges, held in 1031, the Bishop of Cahors made the following statement: "A knight of my diocese being killed in a state of excommunication, I refused to comply with the request of his friends, who solicited me earnestly to give him absolution. My resolution was to make an example of him, in order to strike terror into others. Notwithstanding this, he was buried in a church dedicated to St Peter by some soldiers or knights without any ecclesiastical ceremony, without any leave, and without the assistance of any priest. The next morning his body was found out of the grave, perfectly entire, and without any token of its having been touched. The soldiers who buried him opened the grave and found nothing but the linen which had been wrapped about his body. They then buried him afresh and covered the grave with an enormous quantity of earth and stones. The next day the corpse was found out of the grave again, and there were no symptoms of anyone having been at work. The same thing was repeated five times, and at last they buried him in unconsecrated ground, at a distance from the churchyard, when no further incident occurred."

Rycaut states that the following story was related to him with many asseverations of truth by a grave *Candive Kalois* called Sofronio, a preacher, and a person of no mean repute and learning at Smyrna.

"I knew," he said, "a certain person who, for some misdemeanours committed in the Morea, fled over to the Isle of Milo, where, though he escaped the hand of justice, he could not avoid the sentence of excommunication, from which he could no more fly than from the conviction of his own conscience, or the guilt which ever attended him; for the fatal hour of his death being come, and the sentence of the Church not revoked, the body was carelessly and without solemnity interred in some retired and unfrequented place. In the meantime the relatives of the deceased were much afflicted and anxious for the sad estate of their dead friend, whilst the peasants and islanders were every night affrighted and disturbed with strange and unusual apparitions, which they immediately concluded arose from the grave of the accursed excommunicant, which, according to their custom, they immediately opened, when they found the body uncorrupted, ruddy, and the veins replete with blood. The coffin was furnished with grapes, apples, and nuts, and such fruits as the season afforded. Whereupon, consultation being taken, the Kaloires resolved to make use of the common remedy in those cases, which was to cut and dismember the body into several parts and to boil it in wine, as the approved means of dislodging the evil spirit and disposing the body to a dissolution. But the friends of the deceased, being willing and desirous that the corpse should rest in peace and some ease given to the departed soul, obtained a reprieve from the clergy, and hoped that for a sum of money (they being persons of a competent estate) a release might be purchased from the excommunication under the hand of the Patriarch. In this manner the corpse was for a little while freed from dissection, and letters thereupon sent to Constantinople with this direction, That in case the Patriarch should condescend to take off the excommunication, that the day, hour, and minute that he signed the remission should be inserted in the document. And now the corpse was taken into the church (the country people not being willing it should remain in the field), and prayers and masses were daily said for its dissolution and the pardon of the offender; when one day, after many prayers, supplications, and offerings (as this Sofrino attested to me with many protestations), and whilst he himself was heard performing divine service, on a sudden was heard a rumbling noise in the coffin of the dead party, to the fear and astonishment of all persons then present; which when they had opened they found the body consumed and dissolved as far into its first principles of earth as if it had been several years interred. The hour and minute of this dissolution was immediately noted and precisely observed, which being compared with the date of the Patriarch's release when it was signed at Constantinople, it was found exactly to agree with that moment in which the body returned to its ashes."

In most countries the vampire was regarded as a night-wanderer, but resting in its grave on Friday night, so that the ceremony of absolution had to be performed on that night or during Saturday, because, if the spirit was out on its rambles when the ceremony took place, it was unavailing.

The Sfakians generally believe that the ravages committed by these night-wanderers used in former times to be far more frequent than they are at the present day, and that they have become comparatively rare solely in consequence of the increased zeal and skill possessed by members of the sacerdotal order.

Tournefort relates an entertaining story of a vampire that woefully annoyed the inhabitants of Myconi. Prayers, processions, stabbing with swords, sprinklings of holy water, and even pouring the latter in large quantities down the throat of the refractory *vroucolaca* were all tried in vain. An Albanian who chanced to be at Myconi objected to two of these remedies. It was no wonder the devil continued in, he said, for how could he possibly come through the holy water? And as to swords, they were equally effectual in preventing his exit, for their handles being crosses, he was so much terrified that he dare not pass them. To obviate the latter objection, he recommended that Turkish scymetars should be used. The scymetars were accordingly put in requisition, but the pertinacious devil still retained his hold of the corpse and played his pranks with as much vigour as ever. At length, when all the respectable inhabitants were packing up to take flight to Syra or Tinos, an effectual method of ousting the *vroucolaca* was fortunately suggested. The body was committed to the flames on January 1st, 1701, and the spirit being thus forcibly ejected from its abode, was rendered incapable of doing further mischief.

There is a story told of St Stanislaus raising to life a man who had been dead for three years, whom he called to life in order that he might give evidence on the saint's behalf in a court of justice. After having given his evidence, the resuscitated man returned quietly to his grave.

CHAPTER III
THE VAMPIRE IN BABYLONIA, ASSYRIA, AND GREECE

The belief in the vampire and ghoul was prevalent even in Babylon and Assyria, where it was maintained that the dead could appear again upon earth and seek sustenance from the living. The belief is, in all probability, linked up with the almost universal theory that transfused blood is necessary for revivification. Baths of human blood were anciently prescribed as a possible remedy for leprosy.

Mr R. Campbell Thompson, in his work *The Devils and Evil Spirits of Babylonia*, states that the *Ekimmu* or departed spirit was the soul of the dead person unable to rest, which wandered as a spectre over the earth. "If it found a luckless man who had wandered far from his fellows into haunted places, it fastened upon him, plaguing and tormenting him until such time as a priest should drive it away with exorcisms."

Mr Thompson also gives the translation of the following two tablets, which, it will be seen, contain references to this belief:—

The gods which seize (upon man)

Have come forth from the grave;

The evil wind-gusts

Have come forth from the grave.

To demand the payment of rites and the pouring out of libations,

They have come forth from the grave;

All that is evil in their hosts, like a whirlwind,

Hath come forth from the grave.

The evil Spirit, the evil Demon, the evil Ghost, the evil Devil,

From the earth have come forth;

From the underworld unto the land they have come forth;

In heaven they are unknown,

On earth they are not understood.

They neither stand nor sit

Nor eat nor drink.

INCANTATION

Spirits that minish heaven and earth,

That minish the land,

Spirits that minish the land,

Of giant strength,

Of giant strength and giant tread,

Demons (like) raging bulls, great ghosts,

Ghosts that break through all houses,

Demons that have no shame,

Seven are they!

Knowing no care,

They grind the land like corn;

Knowing no mercy,

They rage against mankind:

They spill their blood like rain,

Devouring their flesh (and) sucking their veins.

Where the images of the gods are, there they quake

In the temple of Nabu, who fertiliseth the shoots of wheat.

They are demons full of violence

Ceaselessly devouring blood.

Invoke the ban against them,

That they no more return to this neighbourhood.

By Heaven be ye exorcised! By Earth be ye exorcised!

Greek Christianity, as already stated, has been credited by many with the origin of the vampire belief, but this contention is hardly borne out by facts. The belief was undoubtedly developed greatly under the influence of the Greek Church, and utilised by the Greek priests as an additional power which they possessed over the people. It did not become prominent in Greece until after the establishment of Christianity, and there are many remarkable stories told of vampire apparitions among the Slavonic races bordering on Greece, as well as among the Arabians. In later times, Father Richard, a French Jesuit of the seventeenth century, went as a missionary to the Archipelago, and has left an account of the islands of Santerini in which he discourses at length upon the *bucolacs* or vampires of that district.

Some Greeks believe that the spectre which appears is not really the soul of the deceased, but an evil spirit which enters his body after the soul of the owner has been withdrawn. Thus Leo Allatius, in describing the belief, says: "The corpse is entered by a demon which is the source of ruin to unhappy men. For frequently emerging from the tomb in the form of that body and roaming about the city and other inhabited places, especially by night it betakes itself to any house it fancies, and, after knocking at the door, addresses one of the inmates in a loud tone. If the person answers he is done for: two days after that he dies. If he does not answer he is safe. In consequence of this, all the people in Chios, if anyone calls to them by night, never reply the first time; for if a second call is given they know that it does not proceed from the *vrykolaka* but from someone else."

In the *Menées des Grecs* it is recorded that an ecclesiastic of Scheti, being excommunicated by his superior for some act of disobedience, quitted the desert and came to Alexandria, where he was apprehended by the governor of the city, stripped of his religious habit, and strongly solicited to sacrifice to the idols of the place. The man bravely resisted the temptation, and was tortured in several ways, till at last they cut off his head, and threw his body out of the city to be devoured by dogs. The next night it was carried away by the Christians, who, having embalmed it and wrapped it up in fine linen, interred it in an honourable part of the church with all the respect due to the remains of a martyr. But at the next celebration of the Mass, upon the deacons crying out aloud as usual, "Let the catechumens and all who do not communicate retire," his grave instantly opened and the martyr retired into the church porch. When Mass was over he came again of his own accord into the grave. Not long afterwards it was revealed by an angel to a holy person, who had continued three days in prayer, that the deceased ecclesiastic had been excommunicated by his superior, and would continue bound till that same superior had reversed the sentence. Upon this a messenger was despatched to the desert after the holy anchorite, who ordered the grave to be opened and absolved the deceased, who, after this, continued in his grave in peace.

Pitton de Tournefort, in his *Voyage into the Levant*, gives the following interesting account: "We were present at a very different scene and one very barbarous at Myconi. The man, whose story we are going to relate, was a peasant of Myconi, naturally ill-natured and quarrelsome; this is a circumstance to be taken notice of in such a case: he was murdered in the fields, nobody knew how or by whom. Two days after his being buried in a chapel in the town it was noised about that he was seen to walk about in the night with great haste, that he tumbled about other people's goods, put out their lamps, gripped them behind, and played a dozen other monkey tricks. At first the story was received with laughter, but the thing was looked upon seriously when the better sort of people began to complain of it: the papás themselves gave credit to the fact, and no doubt had their reasons for so doing; masses were duly said; but for all this the peasant drove his old trade and heeded nothing they could do. After divers meetings of the chief people of the city, of priests and monks, it was gravely concluded that it was necessary in consequence of some musty ceremonial to wait till the ninth day after the interment should be expired.

"On the tenth day they said one Mass in the chapel where the body was laid in order to drive out the demon which they imagined was got into it. After Mass they took up his body and got everything ready for blowing out his heart.... The corpse stunk so abominably that they were obliged to burn frankincense, but the smoke mixing with the exhalations from the carcase increased the stench; every person averred that the blood of the corpse was extremely red. The butcher swore that the body was still warm...."

Pitton concludes the story by ridiculing the theory that this was the body of a vampire or *vroucolaca*.

The practice of burning the body of a suspected or proved vampire does not appear to have found general favour in Greece, doubtless by reason of the fact that the Greeks possessed a religious horror of burning a body on which holy oil had been poured by the priest when performing the last rites upon the dying man.

Leake, whose *Travels in Northern Greece* were published in 1835, says in the fourth volume of that work: "It would be difficult now to meet with an example of the most barbarous of all these superstitions, the Vrukólaka. The name being Illyric, seems to acquit the Greeks of the invention, which was probably introduced into the country by the barbarians of Sclavonic race. Tournefort's description is admitted to be correct. The Devil is supposed to enter the Vrukólaka, who, rising from his grave, torments first his nearest relatives and then others, causing their death or loss of health. The remedy is to dig up the body and if, after it has been exorcised by the priest, the demon still persists in annoying the living, to cut it into small pieces, or, if that be not sufficient, to burn it."

In Crete the belief in vampires—or katalkanás, as the Cretans call them—and their existence and ill-deeds forms a general article of popular belief throughout the island, but is particularly strong in the mountains, and if anyone ventures to doubt it, undeniable facts are brought forward to silence the incredulous.

One of the stories told by the Cretans is as follows: "Once upon a time the village of Kalikráti, in the district of Sfakia, was haunted by a Katakhanás, and the people did not know what man he was or from what part he came. This Katakhanás destroyed both children and full-grown men, and desolated both that village and many others. They had buried him at the church of St George at Kalikráti, and in those times he was regarded as a man of note, and they had built an arch over his grave. Now a certain shepherd, believed to be his mutual Sýnteknos,[1] was tending his sheep and goats near the church, and, on being caught in a shower, he went to the sepulchre that he might be protected from the rain. Afterwards he determined to sleep and pass the night there, and, after taking off his arms, he placed them by the stone which served him as his pillow, crosswise. And people might say that it was on this account that the Katakhanás was not permitted to leave his tomb. During the night, then, as he wished to go out again, that he might destroy men, he said to the shepherd: 'Gossip, get up hence, for I have some business that requires me to come out.' The shepherd answered him not, either the first time, or the second, or the third; further, he knew that the man had become a Katakhanás, and that it was he who had done all those evil deeds. On this account he said to him on the fourth time of his speaking: 'I shall not get up hence, gossip, for I fear you are no better than you should be and may do me some mischief; but if I must get up, swear to me by your winding-sheet that you will not hurt me, and on that I will get up.' And he did not pronounce the proposed words, but said other things; nevertheless, when the shepherd did not suffer him to get up, he swore to him as he wished. On this he got up, and, taking his arms, removed them away from the monument, and the Katakhanás came forth, and, after greeting the shepherd, said to him: 'Gossip, you must not go away, but sit down here; for I have some business which I must go after; but I shall return within the hour, for I have something to say to you.' So the shepherd waited for him.

"And the Katakhanás went a distance of about ten miles, where there was a couple recently married, and he destroyed them. On his return the gossip saw that he was carrying some liver, his hands being moistened with blood; and, as he carried it, he blew into it, just as the butcher does, to increase the size of the liver. And he showed his gossip that it was cooked, as if it had been done on the fire. After this he said: 'Let us sit down, gossip, that we may eat.' And the shepherd pretended to eat it, but only swallowed dry bread, and kept dropping the liver into his bosom. Therefore, when the hour for their separation arrived, the Katakhanás said to the shepherd: 'Gossip, this which you have seen, you must not mention, for if you do, my twenty nails will be fixed in your children and yourself.' Yet the shepherd lost no time, but gave information to the priests and others, and they went to the tomb, and there they found the Katakhanás, just as he had been buried. And all people became satisfied that it was he who had done all the evil deeds. On this account they collected a great deal of wood, and they cast him on it, and burnt him. His gossip was not present, but when the Katakhanás was already half-consumed, he, too, came forward in order that he might enjoy the ceremony. And the Katakhanás cast, as it were, a single spot of blood, and it fell on his foot, which wasted away, as if it had been roasted on a fire. On this account they sifted even the ashes, and found the little finger nail of the Katakhanás unburnt, and burnt it too."

The 22nd formula of the *Cuneiform Inscriptions of Western Asia*, published by Sir Henry Rawlinson and Mr Edwin Norris in 1866, reads:—

The phantom, child of heaven,

which the gods remember,

the *Innin* (kind of hobgoblin) prince

of the lords

the ...

which produces painful fever,

the vampyre which attacks man,

the *Uruku* multifold

upon humanity,

may they never seize him!

[1] That is, related to each other through god-parents. In Crete, those whose god-parents were the same or were connected by ties of kinship were regarded as being in consanguineous relationship, and therefore were unable to contract marriages with each other.

CHAPTER IV
VAMPIRISM IN GREAT AND GREATER BRITAIN

William of Newbury, who flourished about the middle of the twelfth century, relates that in his time a man appeared corporeally in the county of Buckingham for three nights together, to his wife and, afterwards, to his other relatives. The way they took to defend themselves against his frightful visits was to stay up all night and make a noise when they observed that he was coming. Upon this he appeared to several people in broad day. Hereupon the Bishop of Lincoln summoned his council, and was informed that the thing was common in England, and that the only way to stop it which they knew of was to burn the spectre. The bishop did not relish this advice, as he thought the expedient a cruel one; but he wrote out a form of absolution on a scrap of paper and ordered it to be laid on the body of the deceased, which was found to be as fresh and entire as if it had been dead only a day; and from that time the apparition was no more heard of. The author adds that these stories would be thought incredible if several instances of them had not happened in his time, attested by persons of undoubted credit.

The same author mentions a similar story, the *locale* of which was Berwick-on-Tweed, where the body was cut in pieces and burnt. Another vampire was burnt at Melrose Abbey. It was that of a very worldly priest who had been in his lifetime so fond of hunting that he was commonly called a *hundeprest*. A still more remarkable case occurred at a castle in the north of England, where the vampire so frightened all the people that no one ever ventured out of doors between sunset and sunrise. The sons of one of his supposed victims at length opened his grave and pierced his body, from which a great quantity of blood immediately flowed, which plainly proved that a large number of persons had been his victims.

At Waterford, in Ireland, there is a little graveyard under a ruined church near Strongbow's Tower. Legend has it that underneath the ground at this spot there lies a beautiful female vampire still ready to kill those she can lure thither by her beauty.

A vampire story is also related concerning an old Cumberland farmhouse, the victim being a girl whose screams were heard as she was bitten, and who only escaped with her life by thus screaming. In this case the monster was tracked to a vault in the churchyard, where forty or fifty coffins were found open, their contents mutilated and scattered around. One coffin only was untouched, and on the lid being taken off the form was recognised as being that of the apparition which had been seen, and the body was accordingly burnt, when the manifestations ceased.

In vol. iii. of *Borderland* Dr Franz Hartmann gave particulars of some vampire cases which had come under his observation.

"A young lady of G—— had an admirer, who asked her in marriage; but as he was a drunkard she refused and married another. Thereupon the lover shot himself, and soon after that event a vampire, assuming his form, visited her frequently at night, especially when her husband was absent. She could not see him, but felt his presence in a way that could leave no room for doubt. The medical faculty did not know what to make of the case; they called it 'hysterics,' and tried in vain every remedy in the pharmacopœia, until she at last had the spirit exorcised by a man of strong faith."

Another case is that of a miller at D—— who had a healthy servant boy, who soon after entering his service began to fail in health. He had a ravenous appetite, but nevertheless grew daily more feeble. Being interrogated, he at last confessed that a thing which he could not see, but which he could plainly feel, came to him every night and sat upon his stomach, drawing all the life out of him, so that he became paralysed for the time being and could neither move nor cry out. Thereupon the miller agreed to share the bed with the boy, and proposed to him that he should give him a certain sign when the vampire arrived. This was done, and when the sign was given the miller grasped the invisible but very tangible substance that rested upon the boy's stomach, and although it struggled to escape, he grasped it firmly and threw it into the fire. After that the boy recovered his health and there was no repetition of the vampire's visits.

Dr Hartmann adds to this last account: "Those who, like myself, have on innumerable occasions removed astral tumours and thereby cured physical tumours will find the above not incredible nor inexplicable. Moreover, the above accounts do not refer to events of the past, but to persons still living in this country."

The following account is taken from the *Gentleman's Magazine* of July 1851:—

"*Singular Instance of Superstition*, A.D. 1629

"The Case, or, rather, History of a Case that happened in the County of Hereford in the fourth Year of the Reign of King Charles the First, which was taken from a MS. of Serjeant Mainard, who writes thus:

"'I write the evidence which was given, which I and many others heard, and I write it exactly according to what was deposed at the Trial at the Bar in the King's Bench. Johan Norkot, the wife of Arthur Norkot, being murdered, the question arose how she came by her death. The coroner's inquest on view of the body and deposition of Mary Norkot, John Okeman and Agnes, his wife, inclined to find Joan Norkot *felo de se* for they (*i.e.* the witnesses before mentioned) informed the coroner and the jury that she was found dead in the bed and her throat cut, the knife sticking in the floor of the room; that the night before she was so found she went to bed with her child (now plaintiff in this appeal), her husband being absent, and that no other person after such time as she was gone to bed came into the house, the examinants lying in the outer room, and they must needs have seen if any stranger had come in. Whereupon the jury gave up to the coroner their verdict that she was *felo de se*. But afterwards upon rumour in the neighbourhood, and the observation of divers circumstances that manifested she did not, nor according to these circumstances, possibly could, murder herself, thereupon the jury, whose verdict was not drawn into form by the coroner, desired the coroner that the body which was buried might be taken up out of the grave, which the coroner assented to, and thirty days after her death she was taken up, in the presence of the jury and a great number of the people, whereupon the jury changed their verdict. The persons being tried at Hertford Assizes were acquitted, but so much against the evidence that the judge (Harvy) let fall his opinion that it were better an appeal were brought than so foul a murder should escape unpunished.

"'*Anno, paschæ termino, quarto Caroli*, they were tried on the appeal which was brought by the young child against his father, the grandfather and aunt, and her husband Okeman. And because the evidence was so strange I took exact and particular notes of it, which was as followeth, of the matters above mentioned and related, an ancient and grave person, the minister of the parish where the fact was committed, being sworn to give evidence according to custom, deposed, that the body being taken out of the grave thirty days after the party's death and lying on the grave and the four defendants present, they were required each of them to touch the dead body. O.'s wife fell on her knees and prayed God to show token of their innocency, or to some such purpose, but her very words I forget. The appellers did touch the dead body, whereupon the brow of the dead, which was all a livid or carrion colour (that was the verbal expression in the terms of the witness) began to have a dew or gentle sweat, which reached down in drops on the face, and the brow turned and changed to a lively and fresh colour, and the dead opened one of her eyes and shut it again, and this opening the eye was done three several times. She likewise thrust out the ring or marriage finger three times and pulled it in again, and the finger dropt blood from it on the grass.

"'Hyde (Nicholas), Chief Justice, seeming to doubt the evidence, asked the witness: "Who saw this beside yourself?"

"'Witness: "I cannot swear that others saw it; but, my lord," said he, "I believe the whole company saw it, and if it had been thought a doubt, proof would have been made of it, and many would have attested with me."

"'Then the witness observing some admiration in the auditors, he spoke further, "My lord, I am minister of the parish, long knew all the parties, but never had any occasion of displeasure against any of them, nor had to do with them, or they with me, but as their minister. The thing was wonderful to me, but I have no interest in the matter, but am called upon to testify the truth and that I have done."

"'This witness was a reverend person as I guess about seventy years of age. His testimony was delivered gravely and temperately, but to the good admiration of the auditor. Whereupon, applying himself to the Lord Chief Justice, he said, "My lord, my brother here present is minister of the next parish adjacent, and I am assured saw all done as I have affirmed," whereupon that person was also sworn to give evidence, and he deposed the same in every point, viz., the sweat of the brow, the changes of its colour, the opening of the eye, the thrice motion of the finger and drawing it in again; only the first witness deposed that a man dipped his finger in the blood to examine it, and swore he believed it was real blood. I conferred afterwards with Sir Edmund Vowel, barrister at law, and others who concurred in this observation, and for myself, if I were upon my oath, can depose that these depositions, especially of the first witness, are truly here reported in substance.

"'The other evidence was given against the prisoners, viz., against the grandmother of the plaintiff and against Okeman and his wife, that they lay in the next room to the dead person that night, and that none came into the house till they found her dead next morning, therefore if she did not murther herself, they must be the murtherers, and to that end further proof was made. First she lay in a composed manner in her bed, the bed cloaths nothing at all disturbed, and her child by her in the bed. Secondly, her throat was cut from ear to ear and her neck broken, and if she first cut her throat, she could not break her neck in the bed, nor *e contra*. Thirdly, there was no blood in the bed, saving that there was a tincture of blood upon the bolster whereupon her head lay, but no other substance of blood at all. Fourthly, from the bed's head on there was a stream of blood on the floor, till it ponded on the bending of the floor to a very great quantity and there was also another stream of blood on the floor at the bed's feet, which ponded also on the floor to another great quantity but no other communication of blood on either of these places, the one from the other, neither upon the bed, so that she bled in two places severely, and it was deposed that turning up the matte of the bed, there were clotes of congealed blood in the straw of the matte underneath. Fifthly, the bloody knife in the morning was found clinging in the floor a good distance from the bed, but the point of the knife as it stuck in the floor was towards the bed and the haft towards the door. Sixthly, lastly, there was the brand of a thumb and four fingers of a left hand on the dead person's left hand.

"'Hyde, Chief Justice: "How can you know the print of a left hand from the print of a right hand in such a case?"'

"'Witness: "My lord, it is hard to describe it, but if it please the honourable judge (*i.e.* the judge sitting on the bench beside the Chief Justice) to put his left hand on your left hand, you cannot possibly place your right hand in the same posture."'

"'It being done, and appearing so, the defendants had time to make their defence, but gave no evidence to that purpose.

"'The jury departing from the bar and returning, acquitted Okeman and found the other three guilty; who, being severally demanded why judgment should not be pronounced, sayd nothing, but each of them said, "I did not do it." "I did not do it." Judgment was made and the grandmother and the husband executed, but the aunt had the privilege to be spared execution, being with child. I enquired if they confessed anything at execution, but did not as I was told.'

"Thus far the serjeant, afterwards Sir John Mainard, a person of great note and judgment in the law. The paper, of which this is a copy, was found amongst his papers since his death (1690) fair written with his own hand. Mr Hunt of the Temple took a copy of it, gave it me, which I have hereby transcribed.—H. S."

It has been asserted by some writers that the vampire is not to be found in Indian lore and legend, and an attempt has been made to connect this supposititious absence of the blood-sucking demon with the Brahminical and Buddhistic vegetarian and cremation customs. The Indian belief, however, in the existence of vampire spectres is as prevalent as it is in any other country, although the folk-lore and legends concerning them may, perhaps, be more scarce.

Fornari, in his *History of Sorcerers*, relates the following story: "In the beginning of the fifteenth century there lived at Bagdad an aged merchant who had grown wealthy in his business and who had an only son to whom he was tenderly attached. He resolved to marry him to the daughter of another merchant, a girl of considerable fortune, but without any personal attractions. Abul-Hassan, the merchant's son, on being shown the portrait of the lady, requested his father to delay the marriage till he could reconcile his mind to it. Instead, however, of doing this he fell in love with another girl, the daughter of a sage, and he gave his father no peace till he consented to the marriage with the object of his affections. The old man stood out as long as he could, but finding that his son was bent on acquiring the hand of the fair Nadilla, and was equally resolute not to accept the rich and ugly lady, he did what most fathers under such circumstances would do—he acquiesced.

"The wedding took place with great pomp and ceremony, and a happy honeymoon ensued, which might have been happier but for one little circumstance which led to very serious consequences.

"Abul-Hassan noticed that his bride quitted the nuptial couch as soon as she thought her husband was asleep, and did not return to it till an hour before dawn.

"Filled with curiosity, Hassan one night, feigning sleep, saw his wife rise and leave the room. He rose, followed cautiously, and saw her enter the cemetery. By the straggling moonbeams he saw her go into a tomb: he stepped in after her.

"The scene within was horrible. A party of ghouls were assembled with the spoils of the graves they had violated and were feasting on the flesh of the long-buried corpses. His own wife, who, by the way, never touched supper at home, played a no inconsiderable part in the hideous banquet.

"As soon as he could safely escape Abul-Hassan stole back to his bed.

"He said nothing to his bride till next evening when supper was laid, and she declined to eat; then he insisted on her partaking, and when she positively refused he exclaimed roughly: 'Oh yes, you keep your appetite for your feasts with the ghouls.' Nadilla was silent; she turned pale and trembled, and without a word sought her bed. At midnight she rose, fell on her husband with her nails and teeth, tore his throat, and, having opened a vein, attempted to suck his blood; but Abul-Hassan, springing to his feet, threw her down and, with a blow, killed her. She was buried next day.

"Three days after at midnight she reappeared, attacked her husband again, and again attempted to suck his blood. He fled from her and on the morrow opened her tomb, burnt her to ashes and cast the ashes into the Tigris."

There is a monstrous vampire which is said to delight in sucking the blood of children, and is known as a Pănangglan. It has also a liking for sucking the blood of women at childbirth; but, as it is also credited with a dread of thorns, the custom has arisen of placing thorns about the rooms of Indian houses on the occasions of births.

One of the Northern Indian witches—the Jigar-Khor or Liver-eater—is believed to be possessed of the power of being able to steal the liver of another by looks and incantations. A class of witches known as Bhúts are said to have an extraordinary fondness for fish, but also eat rice and all kinds of human food.

Hugh Clifford, in his interesting work *In Court and Kampong*, refers to the "Pĕnangal, that horrible wraith of a woman who has died in childbirth, and who comes to torment small children in the guise of a fearful face and bust with many feet of bloody, trailing entrails in her wake," also of that "weird little white animal, the *Mati-ânak*, that makes beast noises round the graves of children; and of the familiar spirits that men raise up from the corpses of babes who have never seen the light, the tips of whose tongues they bite off and swallow, after the child has been brought back to life by magic agencies."

In the Tamil dream of Harichándra, the frenzied Sandramáti says to the king: "I belong to the race of elves, for I killed thy child in order that I might feed on its delicate flesh." The Vetala is said to feed chiefly on corpses. The Bhúts and other dismal ravenous ghosts, who are dreaded at the moon-wane of the month Katik (October-November), were not supposed to devour men, but only their food.

Then there is the Hántu Sàburo, which chases men into the forest by means of his dogs, and if they are run down he drinks their blood. The Hántu Dondong resides in caves and crevices in rocks. He kills dogs and wild hogs with the sumpitan, and then drinks their blood. The Hántu Parl fastens on to the wound of an injured person and sucks the blood.

Barth, in his *History of Religions* (Hinduism), says that "Siva is identified with *Mrityu*, Death, and his old name *Pacupati*, Lord of herds, acquires the ominous meaning of Master of human cattle. He is chief of the mischievous spirits, of ghouls and vampires that frequent places of execution and those where the dead are buried, and he prowls about with them at nightfall."

Other classes of demons are also known as the *Rakshasas* or the *Pisâchâs*, a word which literally means "flesh-eaters," which Delongchamps has translated as "bloodthirsty savages," but other etymologists actually as "vampires."

The vampire demon is no stranger to Australia. Bonwick, in his *Daily Life of the Tasmanians*, tells us that: "During the whole of the first night after the death of one of their tribe they will sit round the body, using rapidly a low, continuous recitative to prevent the evil spirit from taking it away. This evil spirit was the ghost of an enemy. Fires at night kept off these mischievous beings, which were like the vampires of Europe."

CHAPTER V
VAMPIRISM IN GERMANY AND SURROUNDING COUNTRIES

Germany, the home of modern philosophy, is not free from the belief in the reality of the vampire apparition, although the more horrible forms of the superstition are not frequently encountered. Crosses are, however, frequently erected at the head, or by the side, of graves, even in Protestant cemeteries, in order that their presence may prevent the occupants from being controlled by any demon that might, but for the presence of such charm, take possession of a body; and the *Nachzehrer* is as much dreaded in many parts of Germany as the *Vrykolaka* is in Russia. In some parts of the Kaiser's dominions, food is still buried with the corpse in order to assuage any pangs of hunger that may arise; and even when this is not done, a few grains of corn or rice are scattered upon the grave as a survival of the ancient custom. In Diesdorf it is believed that if money is not placed in the mouth of a dead person at burial, or his name not cut from his shirt, he will, in all probability, become a Nachzehrer, and his ghost issue from the grave in the form of a pig. Another sure preventive of such a calamity is to break the neck of a dead body.

The following story was contributed by Dr Franz Hartmann to the *Occult Review* for September 1909, under the title of "An Authenticated Vampire Story":—

"On June 10th, 1909, there appeared in a prominent Vienna paper (the *Neues Wiener Journal*) a notice saying that the castle of B—— had been burned by the populace, because there was a great mortality among the peasant children, and it was generally believed that this was due to the invasion of a vampire, supposed to be the last Count B——, who died and acquired that reputation. The castle was situated in a wild and desolate part of the Carpathian Mountains, and was formerly a fortification against the Turks. It was not inhabited, owing to its being believed to be in the possession of ghosts; only a wing of it was used as a dwelling for the caretaker and his wife.

"Now it so happened that, when I read the above notice, I was sitting in a coffee-house at Vienna in company with an old friend of mine who is an experienced occultist and editor of a well-known journal, and who had spent several months in the neighbourhood of the castle. From him I obtained the following account, and it appears that the vampire in question was probably not the old Count, but his beautiful daughter, the Countess Elga, whose photograph, taken from the original painting, I obtained. My friend said: 'Two years ago I was living at Hermannstadt, and being engaged in engineering a road through the hills, I often came within the vicinity of the old castle, where I made the acquaintance of the old castellan, or caretaker, and his wife, who occupied a part of the wing of the house, almost separate from the main body of the building. They were a quiet old couple and rather reticent in giving information or expressing an opinion in regard to the strange noises which were often heard at night in the deserted halls, or of the apparitions which the Wallachian peasants claimed to have seen when they loitered in the surroundings after dark. All I could gather was that the old Count was a widower and had a beautiful daughter, who was one day killed by a fall from her horse, and that soon after the old man died in some mysterious manner, and the bodies were buried in a solitary graveyard belonging to a neighbouring village. Not long after their death an unusual mortality was noticed among the inhabitants of the village: several children and even some grown people died without any apparent illness; they merely wasted away; and thus a rumour was started that the old Count had become a vampire after his death. There is no doubt that he was not a saint, as he was addicted to drinking, and some shocking tales were in circulation about his conduct and that of his daughter; but whether there was any truth in them, I am not in a position to say.

"'Afterwards the property came into the possession of ———, a distant relative of the family, who is a young man and officer in a cavalry regiment at Vienna. It appears that the heir enjoyed his life at the capital and did not trouble himself much about the old castle in the wilderness; he did not even come to look at it, but gave his directions by letter to the janitor, telling him merely to keep things in order and to attend to repairs, if any were necessary. Thus the castellan was actually master of the house, and offered its hospitality to me and my friends.

"One evening I and my two assistants, Dr E———, a young lawyer, and Mr W———, a literary man, went to inspect the premises. First we went to the stables. There were no horses, as they had been sold; but what attracted our special attention was an old, queer-fashioned coach with gilded ornaments and bearing the emblems of the family. We then inspected the rooms, passing through some halls and gloomy corridors, such as may be found in any old castle. There was nothing remarkable about the furniture; but in one of the halls there hung in a frame an oil-painting, a portrait, representing a lady with a large hat and wearing a fur coat. We were all involuntarily startled on beholding this picture—not so much on account of the beauty of the lady, but on account of the uncanny expression of her eyes; and Dr E———, after looking at the picture for a short time, suddenly exclaimed: 'How strange! The picture closes its eyes and opens them again, and now it begins to smile!'

"Now Dr E——— is a very sensitive person, and has more than once had some experience in spiritism, and we made up our minds to form a circle for the purpose of investigating this phenomenon. Accordingly, on the same evening we sat around a table in an adjoining room, forming a magnetic chain with our hands. Soon the table began to move and the name *Elga* was spelled. We asked who this Elga was, and the answer was rapped out: 'The lady whose picture you have seen.'

"'Is the lady living?' asked Mr W——. This question was not answered; but instead it was rapped out: 'If W—— desires it, I will appear to him bodily to-night at two o'clock.' W—— consented, and now the table seemed to be endowed with life and manifested a great affection for W——; it rose on two legs and pressed against his breast, as if it intended to embrace him.

"We inquired of the castellan whom the picture represented; but to our surprise he did not know. He said that it was the copy of a picture painted by the celebrated painter Hans Markart of Vienna, and had been bought by the old Count because its demoniacal look pleased him so much.

"We left the castle, and W—— retired to his room at an inn a half-hour's journey distant from that place. He was of a somewhat sceptical turn of mind, being neither a firm believer in ghosts and apparitions nor ready to deny their possibility. He was not afraid, but anxious to see what would come of his agreement, and for the purpose of keeping himself awake he sat down and began to write an article for a journal.

"Towards two o'clock he heard steps on the stairs and the door of the hall opened; there was the rustling of a silk dress and the sound of the feet of a lady walking to and fro in the corridor.

"It may be imagined that he was somewhat startled; but taking courage, he said to himself: 'If this is Elga, let her come in.' Then the door of the room opened and Elga entered. She was most elegantly dressed, and appeared still more youthful and seductive than the picture. There was a lounge on the other side of the table where W—— was writing, and there she silently posted herself. She did not speak, but her looks and gestures left no doubt in regard to her desires and intentions.

"Mr W—— resisted the temptation and remained firm. It is not known whether he did so out of principle or timidity or fear. Be this as it may, he kept on writing, looking from time to time at his visitor and silently wishing that she would leave. At last, after half an hour, which seemed to him much longer, the lady departed in the same manner in which she came.

"This adventure left W—— no peace, and we consequently arranged several sittings at the old castle, where a variety of uncanny phenomena took place. Thus, for instance, once the servant-girl was about to light a fire in the stove, when the door of the apartment opened and Elga stood there. The girl, frightened out of her wits, rushed from the room, tumbling down the stairs in terror with the lamp in her hand, which broke, and came very near to setting her clothes on fire. Lighted lamps and candles went out when brought near the picture, and many other 'manifestations' took place which it would be tedious to describe; but the following incident ought not to be omitted.

"Mr W—— was at that time desirous of obtaining the position as co-editor of a certain journal, and a few days after the above-narrated adventure he received a letter in which a noble lady of high position offered him her patronage for that purpose. The writer requested him to come to a certain place the same evening, where he would meet a gentleman who would give him further particulars. He went, and was met by an unknown stranger, who told him that he was requested by the Countess Elga to invite Mr W—— to a carriage drive, and that she would await him at midnight at a certain crossing of two roads, not far from the village. The stranger then suddenly disappeared.

"Now it seems that Mr W—— had some misgivings about the meeting and drive, and he hired a policeman as detective to go at midnight to the appointed place, to see what would happen. The policeman went and reported next morning that he had seen nothing but the well-known, old-fashioned carriage from the castle, with two black horses, standing there as if waiting for somebody, and that as he had no occasion to interfere, he merely waited until the carriage moved on. When the castellan of the castle was asked, he swore that the carriage had not been out that night, and in fact it could not have been out, as there were no horses to draw it.

"But that is not all, for on the following day I met a friend who is a great sceptic and disbeliever in ghosts, and always used to laugh at such things. Now, however, he seemed to be very serious and said: 'Last night something very strange happened to me. At about one o'clock this morning I returned from a late visit, and as I happened to pass the graveyard of the village, I saw a carriage with gilded ornaments standing at the entrance. I wondered about this taking place at such an unusual hour, and being curious to see what would happen, I waited. Two elegantly dressed ladies issued from the carriage. One of these was young and pretty, but threw at me a devilish and scornful look as they both passed by and entered the cemetery. There they were met by a well-dressed man, who saluted the ladies and spoke to the younger one, saying: "Why, Miss Elga! Are you returned so soon?" Such a queer feeling came over me that I abruptly left and hurried home.'

"This matter has not been explained; but certain experiments which we subsequently made with the picture of Elga brought out some curious facts.

"To look at the picture for a certain time caused me to feel a very disagreeable sensation in the region of the solar plexus. I began to dislike the portrait and proposed to destroy it. We held a sitting in the adjoining room; the table manifested a great aversion to my presence. It was rapped out that I should leave the circle, and that the picture must not be destroyed. I ordered a Bible to be brought in, and read the beginning of the first chapter of St John, whereupon the above-mentioned Mr E—— (the medium) and another man present claimed that they saw the picture distorting its face. I turned the frame and pricked the back of the picture with my penknife in different places, and Mr E——, as well as the other man, felt all the pricks, although they had retired to the corridor.

"I made the sign of the pentagram over the picture, and again the two gentlemen claimed that the picture was horribly distorting its face.

"Soon afterwards we were called away and left that country. Of Elga I heard nothing more."

Thus far goes the account of my friend the editor.

Siegbert's *Chronicle* for the year 858 has the following story: "There appeared this year in the diocese of Mentz a spirit which discovered himself at first by throwing stones and beating against the walls of houses, as if it had been with a great mallet. He then proceeded to speak and reveal secrets, and discovered the authors of several thefts and other matters likely to breed disturbances in the neighbourhood. At last he vented his malice upon one particular person, whom he was industrious in persecuting and making odious to all the neighbours by representing him as the cause of God's anger against the whole village. The spirit never forsook the poor man, but tormented him without intermission, burnt all his corn in the barns, and set every place on fire where he came. The priests attempted to frighten him away by exorcisms, prayers, and holy water; but the spectre answered them with a volley of stones which wounded several of them. When the priests were gone he was heard to bemoan himself and say that he was forced to take refuge in the cowl of one of the priests, who had injured the daughter of a man of consequence in the village. He continued in this manner to infest the village for three years together, and never gave over till he had set every house in it on fire."

CHAPTER VI
VAMPIRISM IN HUNGARY, BAVARIA, AND SILESIA

The Hungarians believe that those who have been passive vampires in life become active vampires after death; that those whose blood has been sucked in life by vampires become themselves vampires after death. In many districts the belief also prevails that the only way to prevent this calamity happening is for the threatened victim to eat some earth from the grave of the attacking vampire, and to smear his own body with blood from the body of that vampire.

That the belief in vampirism is still current in Hungary was evidenced recently. The *Daily Telegraph* of February 15th, 1912, contained the following paragraph: "A Buda-Pesth telegram to the *Messaggero* reports a terrible instance of superstition. A boy of fourteen died some days ago in a small village. A farmer, in whose employment the boy had been, thought that the ghost of the latter appeared to him every night. In order to put a stop to these supposed visitations, the farmer, accompanied by some friends, went to the cemetery one night, stuffed three pieces of garlic and three stones in the mouth, and thrust a stake through the corpse, fixing it to the ground. This was to deliver themselves from the evil spirit, as the credulous farmer and his friends stated when they were arrested."

In 1732, in a village in Hungary, in the space of three months, seventeen persons of different ages died of vampirism, some without being ill, and others after languishing two or three days. It is reported that a girl named Stanoska, daughter of the Heyduk Jotiutso, who went to bed in perfect health, awoke in the middle of the night trembling violently and uttering terrible shrieks, declaring that the son of the Heyduk Millo, who had been dead nine weeks, had nearly strangled her in her sleep. She fell into a languid state and died at the end of three days. Young Millo was exhumed and found to be a vampire.

Calmet, in his work *The Phantom World*, relates the following: "About fifteen years ago a soldier who was billeted at the house of a Haidamaque peasant, on the frontiers of Hungary, as he was one day sitting at table near his host, the master of the house, saw a person he did not know come in and sit down to table also with them. The master of the house was strangely frightened at this, as were the rest of the company. The soldier knew not what to think of it, being ignorant of the matter in question. But the master of the house being dead the very next day, the soldier inquired what it meant. They told him it was the body of the father of the host, who had been dead and buried for ten years, who had thus come to sit down next to him, and had announced and caused his death.

"The soldier informed the regiment of it in the first place, and the regiment gave notice of it to the general officers, who commissioned the Count de Cabreras, captain of the regiment of Alandetti infantry, to make information concerning this circumstance. Having gone to the place with some other officers, a surgeon and an auditor, they heard the depositions of all the people belonging to the house, who decided unanimously that the ghost was the father of the master of the house, and that all the soldier had said and reported was the exact truth, which was confirmed by all the inhabitants of the village.

"In consequence of this the corpse of the spectre was exhumed and found to be like that of a man who had just expired, and his blood like that of a living man. The Count de Cabreras had his head cut off and caused him to be laid again in the tomb. He also took information concerning other similar ghosts: among others, of a man dead more than thirty years who had come back three times to his house at meal-time. The first time he had sucked the blood from the neck of his own brother, the second time from one of his sons, and the third time from one of the servants in the house; and all three died of it instantly and on the spot. Upon this deposition the commissary had this man taken out of his grave, and finding that, like the first, his blood was in a fluidic state like that of a living person, he ordered them to run a large nail into his temple and then to lay him again in the grave.

"He caused a third to be burned who had been buried more than sixteen years and had sucked the blood and caused the death of two of his sons. The commissary having made his report to the general officers, was deputed to the Emperor, who commanded that some officers both of war and of justice, some physicians and surgeons and some learned men should be sent to examine the causes of these extraordinary events. The person who related these particulars to us had heard them from the Count de Cabreras at Fribourg in 1730."

Raufft tells the story of a man named "Peter Plogojowitz, an inhabitant of a village in Hungary called Kisolova, who, after he had been buried more than ten years, appeared by night to several persons in the village, while they were asleep, and squeezed their throats in such a manner that they expired within twenty-four hours. There died in this way no less than nine persons in eight days; and the widow of this Plogojowitz deposed that she herself had been visited by him since his death, and that his errand was to demand his shoes; which frightened her so much that she at once left Kisolova and went to live somewhere else.

"These circumstances determined the inhabitants of the village to dig up the body of Plogojowitz and burn it, in order to put a stop to such troublesome visits. Accordingly they applied to the commanding officer of the Emperor's troops in the district of Gradisca, in the kingdom of Hungary, and to the incumbent of the place, for leave to dig up the corpse. They both made a great many scruples about granting it; but the peasants declared plainly that if they were not permitted to dig up this accursed carcase, which they were fully convinced was a vampire, they would be forced to leave the village and settle where they could.

"The officer who gave this account, seeing that there was no hindering them either by fair means or foul, came in person, accompanied by the minister of Gradisca, to Kisolova, and they were both present at the digging up of the corpse, which they found to be free from any bad smell, and perfectly sound, as if it had been alive, except that the tip of the nose was a little dry and withered. The beard and hair were grown fresh and a new set of nails had sprung up in the room of the old ones that had fallen off. Under the former skin, which looked pale and dead, there appeared a new one, of a natural fresh colour; and the hands and feet were as entire as if they belonged to a person in perfect health. They observed also that the mouth of the vampire was full of fresh blood, which the people were persuaded had been sucked by him from the persons he had killed.

"The officer and the divine having diligently examined into all the circumstances, the people, being fired with fresh indignation, and growing more fully persuaded that this carcase was the real cause of the death of their countrymen, ran immediately to fetch a sharp stake, which being driven into his breast, there issued from the wound, and also from his nose and mouth, a great quantity of fresh, ruddy blood; and something which indicated a sort of life, was observed to come from him. The peasants then laid the body upon a pile of wood, and burnt it to ashes."

Calmet says he was told by M. de Vassimont, who was sent to Moravia by Leopold, first Duke of Lorraine, that he was informed by public report that it was common enough in that country to see men who had died some time before present themselves in a party and sit down to the table with persons of their acquaintance without saying anything, but that nodding to one of the party he would infallibly die some days afterwards. M. de Vassimont received confirmation of this story from several persons, amongst others an old curé who said he had seen more than one instance of it. The priest added that the inhabitants had been delivered from these troublesome spectres owing to the fact that their corpses had been taken up and burned or destroyed in some way or other.

At the beginning of the eighteenth century several vampire investigations were held at the instigation of the Bishop of Olmutz. The village of Liebava was particularly infested, and a Hungarian placed himself on the top of the church tower and just before midnight saw a well-known vampire issue from his tomb, and, leaving his winding-sheet behind him, proceed on his rounds. The Hungarian descended from the tower and took away the sheet and ascended the tower again. When the vampire returned he flew into a great fury because of the absence of the sheet. The Hungarian called to him to come up to the tower and fetch it. The vampire mounted the ladder, but just before he reached the top the Hungarian gave him a blow on the head which threw him down to the churchyard. His assailant then descended, cut off the vampire's head with a hatchet, and from that time the vampire was no more heard of.

In 1672 there dwelt in the market town of Kring, in the Archduchy of Krain, a man named George Grando, who died, and was buried by Father George, a monk of St Paul, who, on returning to the widow's house, saw Grando sitting behind the door. The monk and the neighbours fled. Soon stories began to circulate of a dark figure being seen to go about the streets by night, stopping now and then to tap at the door of a house, but never to wait for an answer. In a little while people began to die mysteriously in Kring, and it was noticed that the deaths occurred in the houses at which the spectred figure had tapped its signal. The widow Grando also complained that she was tormented by the spirit of her husband, who night after night threw her into a deep sleep with the object of sucking her blood. The Supan, or chief magistrate, of Kring decided to take the usual steps to ascertain whether Grando was a vampire. He called together some of the neighbours, fortified them with a plentiful supply of spirituous liquor, and they sallied off with torches and a crucifix.

Grando's grave was opened, and the body was found to be perfectly sound and not decomposed, the mouth being opened with a pleasant smile, and there was a rosy flush on the cheeks. The whole party were seized with terror and hurried back to Kring, with the exception of the Supan. The second visit was made in company with a priest, and the party also took a heavy stick of hawthorn sharpened to a point. The grave and body were found to be exactly as they had been left. The priest kneeled down solemnly and held the crucifix aloft: "O vampire, look at this," he said; "here is Jesus Christ who loosed us from the pains of hell and died for us upon the tree!"

He went on to address the corpse, when it was seen that great tears were rolling down the vampire's cheeks. A hawthorn stake was brought forward, and as often as they strove to drive it through the body the sharpened wood rebounded, and it was not until one of the number sprang into the grave and cut off the vampire's head that the evil spirit departed with a loud shriek and a contortion of the limbs.

Similar stories to this were continually being circulated from the borders of Hungary to the Baltic.

At one time the spectre of a village herdsman near Kodom, in Bavaria, began to appear to several inhabitants of the place, and either in consequence of their fright or from some other cause, every person who had seen the apparition died during the week afterwards. Driven to despair, the peasants disinterred the corpse and pinned it to the ground with a long stake. The same night he appeared again, plunging people into convulsions of fright, and suffocated several of them. Then the village authorities handed the body over to the executioner, who caused it to be carried into a field adjoining the cemetery, where it was burned. The corpse howled like a madman, kicking and tearing as if it had been alive.

When it was run through again with sharp-pointed stakes, before the burning, it uttered piercing cries and vomited masses of crimson blood. The apparition of the spectre ceased only after the corpse had been reduced to ashes.

Fortis, in his *Travels into Dalmatia*, says that the Moslacks have no doubt as to the existence of vampires, and attribute to them, as in Transylvania, the sucking of the blood of infants. Therefore, when a man dies, and he is suspected of vampirism, or of being a *vukodlak*—the term they employ— they cut his hams and prick his whole body with pins, pretending that he will be unable to walk about after this operation has been performed. There are even instances of Moolacchi who, imagining that they may possibly thirst for human blood after death, particularly the blood of children, entreat their heirs, and sometimes even make them promise, to treat them in this manner directly after death.

Dr Henry More, in his *Antidote against Atheism*, argues for the reality of vampires, and relates the following stories.

"A shoemaker of Breslau, in Silesia, in 1591 terminated his life by cutting his throat. His family, however, spread abroad the report that he had died of apoplexy, which enabled them to bury him in the ordinary way and save the disgrace of his being interred as a suicide. Despite this, however, the rumour got abroad that the man had committed suicide. It was also reported that his ghost had been seen at the bedsides of several persons, and the rumours and reports spreading, it was decided by the authorities to disinter the body. It had been buried on September 22nd, 1591, and the grave was opened on April 18th, 1592. The body was found to be entire; it was not in any way putrid, the joints were flexible, there was no ill smell, the wound in the throat was visible and there was no corruption in it. There was also observed what was claimed to be a magical mark on the great toe of the right foot—an excrescence in the form of a rose. The body was kept above ground for six days, during which time the apparitions still appeared. It was then buried beneath the gallows, but the apparition still came to the bedsides of the alarmed inhabitants, pinching and suffocating people, and leaving marks of its fingers plainly visible on the flesh. A fortnight afterwards the body was again dug up, when it was observed to have sensibly increased its size since its last interment. Then the head, arms, and legs of the corpse were cut off; the heart, which was as fresh and entire as that in a freshly killed calf, was also taken out of the body. The whole body thus dismembered was consigned to the flames and the ashes thrown into the river. The apparition was never seen afterwards. A servant of the deceased man was also said to have acted in a similar manner after her death. Her remains were also dug up and burned, and then her apparition ceased to torment the inhabitants."

"Johannes Cuntius, a citizen and alderman of Pentach, in Silesia, when about sixty years of age, died somewhat suddenly, as the result of a kick from his horse. At the moment of his death a black cat rushed into the room, jumped on to the bed, and scratched violently at his face. Both at the time of his death and that of his funeral a great tempest arose—the wind and snow 'made men's bodies quake and their teeth chatter in their heads.' The storm is said to have ceased with startling suddenness as the body was placed under the ground. Immediately after the burial, however, stories began to circulate of the appearance of a phantom which spoke to people in the voice of Cuntius. Remarkable tales were told of the consumption of milk from jugs and bowls, of milk being turned into blood, of old men being strangled, children taken out of cradles, altar-cloths being soiled with blood, and poultry killed and eaten. Eventually it was decided to disinter the body. It was found that all the bodies buried above that of Cuntius had become putrefied and rotten, but his skin was tender and florid, his joints by no means stiff, and when a staff was put between his fingers they closed around it and held it fast in their grasp. He could open and shut his eyes, and when a vein in his leg was punctured the blood sprang out as fresh as that of a living person. This happened after the body had been in the grave for about six months. Great difficulty was experienced when the body was cut up and dismembered, by the order of the authorities, by reason of the resistance offered; but when the task was completed, and the remains consigned to the flames, the spectre ceased to molest the natives or interfere with their slumbers or health."

CHAPTER VII
VAMPIRISM IN SERVIA AND BULGARIA

The document which gives the particulars of the following remarkable story is signed by three regimental surgeons and formally countersigned by the lieutenant-colonel and sub-lieutenant, and bears the date June 7th, 1732, with the address Meduegna, near Belgrade.

"In the spring of 1727 there returned from the Levant to the village of Meduegna, near Belgrade, one Arnod Paole, who, in a few years' military service and varied adventure, had amassed enough to purchase a cottage and an acre or two of land in his native place, where he gave out that he meant to pass the remainder of his days. He kept his word. Arnod had yet scarcely reached the prime of manhood; and though he must have encountered the rough as well as the smooth of life, and have mingled with many a wild and reckless companion, yet his natural good disposition and honest principles had preserved him unscathed in the scenes he had passed through. At all events, such were the thoughts expressed by his neighbours as they discussed his return and settlement among them in the stube of the village hof. Nor did the frank and open countenance of Arnod, his obliging habits and steady conduct, argue their judgments incorrect. Nevertheless, there was something occasionally noticeable in his ways, a look and tone that betrayed inward disquiet. He would often refuse to join his friends, or on some sudden plea abruptly quit their society. And he still more unaccountably, and it seemed systematically, avoided meeting his pretty neighbour, Nina, whose father occupied the next farm to his own. At the age of seventeen Nina was as charming a picture of youth, cheerfulness, innocence, and confidence as you could have seen in all the world. You could not look into her limpid eye, which steadily returned your gaze, without seeing to the bottom of the pure and transparent spring of her thoughts. Why then did Arnod shrink from meeting her? He was young; had a little property; had health and industry; and he had told his friends he had formed no ties in other lands. Why then did he avoid the fascination of the pretty Nina, who seemed a being made to chase from any brow the clouds of gathering care? But he did so, yet less and less resolutely, for he felt the charm of her presence. Who could have done otherwise? And how long he resisted the impulse of his fondness for the innocent girl who sought to cheer his fits of depression!

"And they were to be united—were betrothed; yet still the anxious gloom would fitfully overcast his countenance, even in the sunshine of those hours.

"'What is it, dear Arnod, that makes you sad? It cannot be on my account, I know, for you were sad before you noticed me; and that, I think surely, first made me notice you.'

"'Nina,' he answered, 'I have done, I fear, a great wrong in trying to gain your affections. Nina, I have a fixed impression that I shall not live; yet, knowing this, I have selfishly made my existence necessary to your happiness.'

"'How strangely you talk, dear Arnod! Who in the village is stronger and healthier than you? You feared no danger when you were a soldier. What danger do you fear as a villager of Meduegna?'

"'It haunts me, Nina.'

"'But, Arnod, you were sad before you thought of me. Did you then fear to die?'

"'Oh, Nina, it is something worse than death.' And his vigorous frame shook with agony.

"'Arnod, I conjure you, tell me.'

"'It was in Cossova this fate befell me. Here you have hitherto escaped the terrible scourge. But there they die, and the dead visit the living. I experienced the first frightful visitation, and I fled; but not till I had sought his grave and executed the dread expiation from the vampire.'

"Nina's blood ran cold. She stood horror-stricken. But her young heart soon mastered her first despair. With a touching voice she spoke: 'Fear not, dear Arnod; fear not now. I will be your shield, or I will die with you!'

"And she encircled his neck with her gentle arms, and returning hope shone, Iris-like, amid her falling tears. Afterwards they found a reasonable ground for banishing or allaying their apprehension in the lengthy time which had elapsed since Arnod left Cossova, during which no fearful visitant had again approached him; and they fondly protested *that* gave them security.

"One day about a week after this conversation Arnod missed his footing when on the top of a loaded hay-waggon, and fell from it to the ground. He was picked up insensible, and carried home, where, after lingering a short time, he died. His interment, as usual, followed immediately. His fate was sad and premature. But what pencil could paint Nina's grief?

"Twenty or thirty days after his decease, several in the neighbourhood complained that they were haunted by the deceased Arnod; and what was more to the purpose, four of them died. The evil looked at sceptically was bad enough, but aggravated by the suggestions of superstition it spread a panic through the whole district. To allay the popular terror, and, if possible, to get at the root of the evil, a determination was come to publicly to disinter the body of Arnod, with the view of ascertaining whether he really was a vampire, and, in that event, of treating him conformably. The day fixed for these proceedings was the fortieth after his burial.

"It was on a grey morning in early August that the commission visited the cemetery of Meduegna, which, surrounded with a wall of stone, lies sheltered by the mountain that, rising in undulating green slopes, irregularly planted with fruit-trees, ends in an abrupt craggy ridge, covered with underwood. The graves were, for the most part, neatly kept, with borders of box, or something like it, and flowers between, and at the head of most, a small wooden cross, painted black, bearing the name of the tenant. Here and there a stone had been raised. One of terrible height, a single narrow slab, ornamented with grotesque Gothic carvings, dominated over the rest. Near this lay the grave of Arnod Paole, towards which the party moved. The work of throwing out the earth was begun by the grey, careful old sexton, who lived in the Leichenhaus beyond the great crucifix. Near the grave stood two military surgeons or *feldscherers* from Belgrade, and a drummer-boy, who held their case of instruments. The boy looked on with keen interest; and when the coffin was exposed and rather roughly drawn out of the grave, his pale face and bright, intent eye showed how the scene moved him. The sexton lifted the lid of the coffin; the body had become inclined to one side. Then, turning it straight: 'Ha, ha! What? Your mouth not wiped since last night's work?'

"The spectators shuddered; the drummer-boy sank forward, fainting, and upset the instrument case, scattering its contents; the senior surgeon, infected with the horror of the scene, repressed a hasty exclamation. They threw water on the drummer-boy and he recovered, but would not leave the spot. Then they inspected the body of Arnod. It looked as if it had not been dead a day. After handling it, the scarfskin came off, but below were *new skin and new nails*! How could they have come there but from this foul feeding? The case was clear enough: there lay before them the thing they dreaded—the vampire! So, without more ado, they simply drove a stake through poor Arnod's chest, whereupon a quantity of blood gushed forth, and the corpse uttered a dreadful groan.

"'Murder! Murder!' shrieked the drummer-boy, as he rushed wildly, with convulsed gestures, from the scene."

The body of Arnod was then burnt to ashes, which were returned to the grave. The authorities further staked and burnt the bodies of the four others who were supposed to have been infected by Arnod. No mention is made of the state in which they were found. The adoption of these decisive measures failed, however, entirely to extinguish the evil, which continued still to hang about the village. About five years afterwards it had again become very rife, and many died through it; whereupon the authorities determined to make another and a complete clearance of the vampire in the cemetery, and with that object they had all the graves, to which suspicion attached, opened, and their contents officially anatomised, and the following are abridgments of the medical reports:—

1. A woman of the name of Stana, twenty years of age, who had died three months before, of a three days' illness following her confinement. She had before her death avowed that she had *anointed* herself with the blood of a vampire, to liberate herself from his persecution. Nevertheless she had died. Her body was entirely free from decomposition. On opening it the chest was found filled with recently effused blood, and the bowels had exactly the appearance of sound health. The skin and nails of her hands and feet were loose and came off, but underneath were new skin and nails.

2. A woman of the name of Miliza, who had died at the end of a three months' illness. The body had been buried ninety and odd days. In the chest was liquid blood. The viscera were as in the former instance. The body was declared by a heyduk, who recognised it, to be in better condition and fatter than it had been in the woman's legitimate lifetime.

3. The body of a child eight years old, that had likewise been buried ninety days; it was in the vampire condition.

4. The son of a heyduk, named Milloc, sixteen years old. The body had lain in the grave nine weeks. He had died after three days' indisposition, and was in the condition of a vampire.

5. Joachim, likewise the son of a heyduk, seventeen years old. He had died after three days' illness; had been buried eight weeks and some days; was found in the vampire state.

6. A man of the name of Rusha, who had died of an illness of ten days' duration and had been six weeks buried, in whom likewise fresh blood was found in the chest.

7. The body of a girl ten years of age who had died two months before. It was likewise in the vampire state, perfectly undecomposed, with blood in the chest.

8. The body of the wife of one Hadnuck, buried seven weeks before; and that of her infant eight weeks old, buried only twenty-one days. They were both in a state of decomposition, though buried in the same ground and closely adjoining the others.

9. A servant, by name Rhade, twenty-three years of age; he had died after an illness of three months' duration, and the body had been buried five weeks. It was in a state of decomposition.

10. The body of the heyduk Stanco, sixty years of age, who had died six weeks previously. There was much blood and other fluid in the chest and abdomen, and the body was in a vampire condition.

11. Millac, a heyduk, twenty-five years old. The body had been in the earth six weeks. It was also in the vampire condition.

12. Stanjoika, the wife of a heyduk, twenty years old; had died after an illness of three days, and had been buried eighteen. The countenance was florid. There was blood in the chest and in the heart. The viscera were perfectly sound, the skin remarkably flush.

The vampire tradition in its original loathsomeness, however, is to be found only in the Bulgarian provinces, whither the knowledge of the superstition was first imported from Dalmatia and Albania. In the former country the vampire is known by the name of *wukodlak*.

St Clair and Brophy, in their work on Bulgaria, state that in Bulgaria the vampire is no longer a dead body possessed by a demon, but a soul in revolt against the inevitable principle of corporeal death. He is detected by a hole in the tombstone which is placed over his grave, which hole is filled up by the medicine man with dirt mixed with poisonous herbs.

Vampirism is claimed to be hereditary as well as epidemic and endemic, and vampires are also stated to be capable of exercising considerable physical force. Stories are told of men who have had their jaws broken, as well as their limbs, as the result of their struggles with vampires.

About 1863 there was a local epidemic of vampirism in one of the villages of Bulgaria, when the place became so infested by them that the inhabitants were forced to assemble together in two or three houses, burn candles at night, and watch by turns in order to avoid the assaults made by the Obours, who lit up the streets with their sparkles. Some of the most enterprising of these threw their shadows on the walls of the rooms where the peasants were assembled through fear, while others howled and shrieked and swore outside the door, entered the abandoned houses, spat blood on the floors, turned everything topsy-turvy, and smeared everything, even the pictures of the saints, with cow-dung, until an old lady, suspected of witchcraft, discovered and laid the troublesome spirit, and afterwards the village was free.

When the Bulgarian vampire has finished his forty days' apprenticeship to the world of shadows, he rises from the tomb in bodily form, and is able to pass himself off as a human being living in the natural manner.

In Slavonic countries the vampire is said to be possessed of only one nostril, but is credited with possessing a sharp point at the end of his tongue, like the sting of a bee.

In Bulgaria one method of abolishing the vampire is said to be by bottling him. The sorcerer, armed with the picture of some saint, lies in ambush until he sees the vampire pass, when he pursues him with his picture. The vampire takes refuge in a tree or on the roof of a house, but his persecutor follows him up with the talisman, driving him away from all shelter in the direction of a bottle specially prepared, in which is placed some favourite food of the vampire. Having no other alternative, he enters this prison, and is immediately fastened down with a cork on the interior of which is a fragment of an eikon or holy picture. The bottle is then thrown into the fire and the vampire disappears for ever.

In Bulgaria the vampire does not invariably seem to have the thirst for human blood, unless there happens to be a shortage in his human food—a distinction which marks him from the species found in other countries.

CHAPTER VIII
VAMPIRE BELIEF IN RUSSIA

The Slavonic belief in vampires is one of the characteristic features of their creed.

The Little Russians hold that, if the vampire's hands have grown numb from remaining long crossed in the grave, he makes use of his teeth, which are like steel. When he has gnawed his way with these through all obstacles, he first destroys the babies he finds in a house, and afterwards the older inmates. If fine salt be scattered on the floor of a room, the vampire's footsteps may be traced to his grave, in which he will be found resting with rosy cheek and gory mouth.

The Kashoubes say that when a *vieszcy*, as they call a vampire, wakes from his sleep within the grave he begins to gnaw his hands and feet, and as he gnaws, first his relatives, and then his neighbours, sicken and die. When he has finished his own store of flesh, he rises at midnight and destroys cattle or climbs a belfry and sounds the bell. All who hear the ill-omened tones will soon die. Generally he sucks the blood of sleepers.

Ralston, in his *Songs of the Russian People*, says that it is in the Ukraine and in White Russia—so far as the Russian Empire is concerned—that traditions are most rife about this ghastly creation of morbid fancy, and that the Little Russians attribute the birth of a vampire to an unholy union between a witch and a werwolf or a devil.

He relates the following as a specimen of the vampire stories prevalent in the country:—

"A peasant was driving past a graveyard after it had grown dark. After him came running a stranger, dressed in a red shirt and a new jacket, who said: 'Stop! Take me as your companion.'

"'Pray take a seat.'

"They enter a village, drive up to this and that house. Though the gates are wide open, yet the stranger says, 'Shut tight!' for on those gates crosses have been branded. They drive on to the very last house: the gates are barred, and from them hangs a padlock weighing a score of pounds; but there is no cross there, and the gates open of their own accord.

"They go into the house: there on the bench lie two sleepers—an old man and a lad. The stranger takes a pail, places it near the youth, and strikes him on the back; immediately the back opens, and forth flows rosy blood. The stranger fills the pail full and drinks it dry. Then he fills another pail with blood from the old man, slakes his brutal thirst, and says to the peasant: 'It begins to grow light! Let us go back to my dwelling.'

"In a twinkling they find themselves at the graveyard. The vampire would have clasped the peasant in his arms, but luckily for him the cocks begin to crow, and the corpse disappears. The next morning, when folks come and look, the old man and the lad are dead."

According to the Servians and Bulgarians, unclean spirits enter into the corpses of malefactors and other evilly disposed persons, who then become vampires. In some places the jumping of a boy over the corpse is considered as fatal as that of a cat.

There is a story told of a mother who lived in Saratof who cursed her son, and his body remained free from corruption after burial for a hundred years. When it was disinterred, his aged mother, who is said to have been still alive, pronounced his pardon, and, at that very moment, the corpse crumbled into dust.

The Russians say that, when driving a stake into the body of a vampire, this must be done by one single blow, as a second blow will reanimate the corpse.

One group of Russian stories relate to the sudden resuscitation shortly after death of wizards and witches at midnight possessed with the longing to eat the flesh of the watchers around the bier. The stories go that the body of the suspected witch was generally enclosed in a coffin which was secured with iron bands and carried to the church, and a watcher was appointed to read aloud from the Scriptures over the coffin right through each night until burial. It was also the duty of the watcher to draw on the floor a magic circle, within which he must stand and hold in his hand a hammer, the ancient weapon of the thunder-god. If the suspicion that the individual was a wizard or witch was a correct one, a mighty wind would arise one night about twelve o'clock, the iron bands of the coffin would give way with a terrible crash, the coffin-lid fall off, and the corpse leap forth and, uttering a terrible screech, rush at the watcher, who, if he had not taken the prescribed precautions, would fall a victim to the monster, and in the morning there would be nothing left of him but his bare bones. The following story of this character is contained in the records of the Kharkof government:—

"Once, in the days of old, there died a terrible sinner. His body was taken into the church, and the sacristan was told to read some psalms over him. He took the precaution to catch a cock and carry it with him to the church. At midnight the dead man leaped from his coffin, opened wide his jaws, and rushed at his victim; but, at that moment, the sacristan gave the bird a hard pinch. The cock uttered his usual crow, and at the same moment the dead man fell backwards to the ground a numb, motionless corpse."

The following story is also given by Ralston in his collection of Russian folk-stories:—

The Coffin Lid

"A moujik was driving along one night with a load of pots. His horse grew tired, and all of a sudden it came to a standstill alongside of a graveyard. The moujik unharnessed his horse and set it free to graze; meanwhile he laid himself down on one of the graves. But somehow he didn't go to sleep.

"He remained there some time. Suddenly the grave began to open beneath him; he felt the movement and sprang to his feet. The grave having opened, out of it came a corpse, wrapped in a white shroud, and holding a coffin lid. He ran to the church, laid the coffin lid at the door, and then set off for the village.

"The moujik was a daring fellow. He picked up the coffin lid and remained standing beside his cart, waiting to see what would happen. After a short delay the dead man came back, and was going to snatch up his coffin lid—but it was not to be seen. Then the corpse began to track it out, traced it up to the moujik, and said: 'Give me my lid; if you don't, I'll tear you to bits!'

"'And my hatchet—how about that?' answered the moujik. 'Why, it's I who'll be chopping you into small pieces!'

"'Do give it back to me, good man!' begs the corpse.

"'I'll give it when you tell me where you've been and what you've done.'

"'Well, I've been in the village, and there I've killed a couple of youngsters.'

"'Well, then, tell me how they can be brought back to life.'

"The corpse reluctantly made answer: 'Cut off the left skirt of my shroud. Take it with you, and when you come into the house where the youngsters were killed, pour some live coals into a pot and put the piece of the shroud in with them, and then lock the door. The lads will be revived by the smoke immediately.'

"The moujik cut off the left skirt of the shroud and gave up the coffin lid. The corpse went to its grave—the grave opened. But just as the dead man was descending into it, all of a sudden the cocks began to crow, and he had not time to get properly covered over. One end of the coffin lid remained standing out of the ground.

"The moujik saw all this and made a note of it. The day began to dawn; he harnessed his horse and drove into the village. In one of the houses he heard cries and wailing. In he went—there lay two dead lads.

"'Don't cry,' said he; 'I can bring them to life.'

"'Do bring them to life, kinsman,' said their relatives. 'We'll give you half of all we possess.'

"The moujik did everything as the corpse had instructed him, and the lads came back to life. Their relatives were delighted, but they immediately seized the moujik and bound him with cords, saying: 'No, no, trickster! We'll hand you over to the authorities. Since you know how to bring them back to life, maybe it was you who killed them!'

"'What are you thinking about, true believers? Have the fear of God before your eyes!' cried the moujik.

"Then he told them everything that had happened to him during the night. Well, they spread the news through the village, and the whole population assembled and stormed into the graveyard. They found the grave from which the dead man had come out; they tore it open, and they drove an aspen stake right into the heart of the corpse, so that it might no more rise up and slay. But they rewarded the moujik handsomely, and sent him home with great honour."

The Soldier and the Vampire

"A certain soldier was allowed to go home on furlough. Well, he walked and walked and walked, and after a time he began to draw near to his native village. Not far off from that village lived a miller in his mill. In old times, the soldier had been very intimate with him: why shouldn't he go and see his friend? He went. The miller received him cordially, and at once brought out liquor; and the two began drinking and chattering about their ways and doings. All this took place towards nightfall, and the soldier stopped so long at the miller's that it grew quite dark.

"When he proposed to start for his village, his host exclaimed: 'Spend the night here, trooper; it is very late now, and perhaps you may run into mischief.'

"'How so?'

"'God is punishing us! A terrible warlock has died among us, and by night he rises from his grave, wanders through the village, and does such things as bring fear upon the very bailiffs; and so how could you help being afraid of him?'

"'Not a bit of it! A soldier is a man who belongs to the Crown, and Crown property cannot be drowned in water or burned in fire. I will be off. I am tremendously anxious to see my people as soon as possible.'

"Off he set. His road lay in front of a graveyard. On one of the graves he saw a great fire blazing. What is that? Then he said: 'Let's have a look.' When he drew near, he saw that the warlock was sitting at the fire, sewing boots.

"'Hail, brother!' calls out the soldier.

"The warlock looked up and said: 'What have you come here for?'

"'Why, I wanted to see what you were doing.'

"The warlock threw his work aside and invited the soldier to a wedding.

"'Come along, brother,' says he; 'let's enjoy ourselves. There is a wedding going on in the village.'

"'Come along,' says the soldier.

"They came to where the wedding was; they were given drink, and treated with the utmost hospitality. The warlock drank and drank, revelled and revelled, and then grew angry. He chased all the guests and relatives out of the house, threw the wedded pair into a slumber, took out two phials and an awl, pierced the hands of the bride and bridegroom with the awl, and began drawing off their blood. Having done this, he said to the soldier: 'Now, let's be off.'

"Accordingly, they went off. On the way the soldier said: 'Tell me, why did you draw off their blood in those phials?'

"'Why, in order that the bride and bridegroom might die. To-morrow morning no one will be able to wake them. I alone know how to bring them back to life.'

"'How's that managed?'

"'The bride and bridegroom must have cuts made in their heels, and some of their blood must then be poured back into these wounds. I've got the bridegroom's blood stowed away in my right-hand pocket, and the bride's in my left.'

"The soldier listened to this without letting a single word escape him. Then the warlock began boasting again.

"'Whatever I wish,' says he, 'that I can do.'

"'I suppose it's quite impossible to get the better of you,' says the soldier.

"'Impossible? If anyone were to make a pyre of aspen boughs, a hundred loads of them, and were to burn me on that pyre, then he'd be able to get the better of me. Only he'd have to look sharp in burning me, for snakes and worms and different kinds of reptiles would creep out of my inside, and crows and magpies and jackdaws would come flying up. All these must be caught and flung on the pyre. If so much as a single maggot were to escape, then there'd be no help for it. In that maggot I should slip away.'

"The soldier listened to all this and did not forget it. He and the warlock talked and talked, and at last they arrived at the grave.

"'Well, brother,' said the warlock, 'now I'll tear you to pieces, otherwise you'll be telling all this.'

"'What are you talking about? Don't you deceive yourself, for I serve God and the Empire.'

"The warlock gnashed his teeth, howled aloud, and sprang at the soldier, who drew his sword and began laying about him with sweeping blows. They struggled and struggled; the soldier was all but at the end of his strength. 'Ah,' thinks he, 'I'm a lost man, and all for nothing!' Suddenly the cocks began to crow. The warlock fell lifeless to the ground.

"The soldier took the phials of blood out of the warlock's pockets, and went to the house of his own people. When he had got there and exchanged greetings with his relatives, they said: 'Did you see any disturbance, soldier?'

"'No, I saw none.'

"'There, now! Why, we've a terrible piece of work going on in the village. A warlock has taken to haunting it.'

"After talking a while they lay down to sleep. The next morning the soldier awoke and began asking: 'I'm told you've got a wedding going on somewhere here.'

"'There was a wedding in the house of a rich moujik,' replied his relatives, 'but the bridegroom has died this very night—what from nobody knows.'

"'Where does this moujik live?'

"They showed him the house. Thither he went without speaking a word. When he got there he found the whole family in tears.

"'What are you mourning about?' says he.

"'Such and such is the state of things, soldier,' say they.

"'I can bring your young people to life again. What will you give me if I do?'

"'Take what you like, even were it half of what we have got.'

"The soldier did as the warlock had instructed him, and brought the young people back to life. Instead of weeping there began to be happiness and rejoicing: the soldier was hospitably treated and well rewarded. Then—left about face! Off he marched to Starosta and told the burgomaster to call the peasants together and to get ready a hundred loads of aspen wood. Well, they took the wood into the graveyard, dragged the warlock out of his grave, placed him on the pyre, and set it in flames. The warlock began to burn. His corpse burst, and out of it came snakes, worms, and all kinds of reptiles, and up came flying crows, magpies, and jackdaws. The peasants knocked them down and flung them into the fire, not allowing so much as a single maggot to creep away! And so the warlock was thoroughly consumed, and the soldier collected his ashes and strewed them to the winds. From that time there was peace in the village.

"The soldier received the thanks of the whole community."

In Russian folk-lore there is a class of demons known as "heart devourers," who touch their victim with an aspen or other twig credited with magical properties; the heart then falls out and may be replaced by some baser one. There is a Moscovian story in which a hero awakes with the heart of a hare, the work of a demon while the man was asleep. He remained a coward for the rest of his life. In another instance a very quiet, reserved, inoffensive peasant received a cock's heart in exchange for his own, and afterwards was for ever crowing like a healthy bird.

The following is taken from the *Lettres Juives* of 1738:—

"In the beginning of September there died in the village of Kisilova, three leagues from Graditz, an old man who was sixty-two years of age. Three days after he had been buried, he appeared in the night to his son, and asked him for something to eat; the son having given him something, he ate and disappeared. The next day the son recounted to his neighbours what had happened. That night the father did not appear, but the following night he showed himself and asked for something to eat. They know not whether the son gave him anything or not; but the next day he was found dead in his bed. On the same day, five or six persons fell suddenly ill in the village, and died one after the other in a few days.

"The officer or bailiff of the place, when informed of what had happened, sent an account of it to the tribunal of Belgrade, which despatched to the village two of these officers and an executioner to examine into this affair. The imperial officer from whom we have this account repaired thither from Graditz to be a witness of what took place.

"They opened the graves of those who had been dead six weeks. When they came to that of the old man, they found him with his eyes open, having a fine colour, with natural respiration, nevertheless motionless as the dead: whence they concluded that he was most undoubtedly a vampire. The executioner drove a stake into his heart; they then raised a pile and reduced the corpse to ashes. No mark of vampirism was found either on the corpse of the son or on the others."

The following story is told by Madame Blavatsky in *Isis Unveiled*, who states that she had the account from an eye-witness of the occurrence:—

"About the beginning of the nineteenth century there occurred in Russia one of the most frightful cases of vampirism on record. The governor of the province of Tch—— was a man of about sixty years of age, of a cruel and jealous disposition. Clothed with despotic authority, he exercised it without stint, as his brutal instincts prompted. He fell in love with the pretty daughter of a subordinate officer. Although the girl was betrothed to a young man whom she loved, the tyrant forced her father to consent to his having her marry him; and the poor victim, despite her despair, became his wife. His jealous disposition soon exhibited itself. He beat her, confined her to her room for weeks together, and prevented her seeing anyone except in his presence. He finally fell sick and died. Finding his end approaching, he made her swear never to marry again, and with fearful oaths threatened that in case she did he would return from his grave and kill her. He was buried in the cemetery across the river, and the young widow experienced no further annoyance until, getting the better of her fears, she listened to the importunities of her former lover, and they were again betrothed.

"On the night of the customary betrothal feast, when all had retired, the old mansion was aroused by shrieks proceeding from her room. The doors were burst open, and the unhappy woman was found lying on her bed in a swoon. At the same time a carriage was heard rumbling out of the courtyard. Her body was found to be black and blue in places, as from the effect of pinches, and from a slight puncture in her neck drops of blood were oozing. Upon recovering, she stated that her deceased husband had suddenly entered her room, appearing exactly as in life, with the exception of a dreadful pallor; that he had upbraided her for her inconstancy, and then beaten and pinched her most cruelly. Her story was disbelieved; but the next morning the guard stationed at the other end of the bridge which spans the river reported that just before midnight a black coach-and-six had driven furiously past without answering their challenge.

"The new governor, who disbelieved the story of the apparition, took nevertheless the precaution of doubling the guards across the bridge. The same thing happened, however, night after night, the soldiers declaring that the toll-bar at their station near the bridge would rise of itself, and the spectral equipage would sweep past them, despite their efforts to stop it. At the same time every night the watchers, including the widow's family and the servants, would be thrown into a heavy sleep; and every morning the young victim would be found bruised, bleeding, and swooning as before. The town was thrown into consternation. The physicians had no explanations to offer; priests came to pass the night in prayer, but as midnight approached, all would be seized with the same terrible lethargy. Finally the archbishop of the province came and performed the ceremony of exorcism in person. On the following morning the governor's widow was found worse than ever. She was now brought to death's door.

"The governor was finally driven to take the severest measures to stop the ever-increasing panic in the town. He stationed fifty Cossacks along the bridge, with orders to stop the spectral carriage at all hazards. Promptly at the usual hour it was heard and seen approaching from the direction of the cemetery. The officer of the guard and a priest bearing a crucifix planted themselves in front of the toll-bar and together shouted: 'In the name of God and the Czar, who goes there?' Out of the coach was thrust a well-remembered head, and a familiar voice responded: 'The Privy Councillor of State and Governor C——!' At the same moment the officer, the priest, and the soldiers were flung aside, as by an electric shock, and the ghostly equipage passed them before they could recover breath.

"The archbishop then resolved as a last expedient to resort to the time-honoured plan of exhuming the body and driving an oaken stake through its heart. This was done with great religious ceremony in the presence of the whole populace. The story is that the body was found gorged with blood, and with red cheeks and lips. At the instant that the first blow was struck upon the stake a groan issued from the corpse and a jet of blood spouted high into the air. The archbishop pronounced the usual exorcism, the body was reinterred, and from that time no more was heard of the vampire."

CHAPTER IX
MISCELLANEA

Voltaire was surprised that in the enlightened eighteenth century there should still be people found who believed in the reality of vampires, and that the doctors of the Sorbonne should give their *imprimatur* to a dissertation on these unpleasant creatures. Yet from 1730 to 1735 the subject of vampirism formed a principal topic of conversation, and may be said to have been a mania all over the world, with Europe as a particular centre. Pamphlets on the subject streamed from the press, the newspapers vied with one another in recording fresh achievements of the spectres, and though the philosophers scoffed at and ridiculed the belief, yet sovereigns sent officers and commissioners to report upon their misdeeds. The favourite scenes of their exploits were Hungary, Poland, Silesia, Bohemia, and Moravia, and in those countries a vampire haunted and tormented almost every village.

In some parts of Scandinavia a singular method was adopted for getting rid of vampires, viz. by instituting judicial proceedings against them. Inhabitants were regularly summoned to attend the inquest; a tribunal was constituted; charges were preferred with the usual legal formalities, accusing them of molesting the houses and introducing death among the inhabitants; and at the end of the proceedings judgment was proclaimed. The priest then entered with holy water, Mass was celebrated, and it was held that complete conquest had been gained over the goblins.

Sir Walter Scott, in his translation of *Eyrbyggia Saga*, relates a traditional story of several vampires who committed dreadful ravages in Iceland in the year 1000, so that in a household of thirty servants no less than eighteen died.

Saxo Grammaticus, the earliest chronicler and writer upon Danish history and folk-lore, in his *Danish History* (book i.), dealing with the origin of the Danes, relates the following story:—

One Mith-othin, who was famous for his juggling tricks, was quickened, as though by an inspiration from on High, to seize the opportunity of feigning to be a god; and, wrapping the minds of the barbarians in fresh darkness, he led them by the renown of his jugglings to pay holy observance to his name. He said that the wrath of the gods could never be appeased nor the outrage to their deity expiated by mixed and indiscriminate sacrifices, and, therefore, forbade that prayers for this end should be put up without distinction, appointing to each of those above his especial drink-offering. But when Odin was returning, he cast away all help of jugglings, went to Finland to hide himself, and was there attacked and slain by the inhabitants. Even in his death his abominations were made manifest, for those who came nigh his barrow were cut off by a kind of sudden death; and, after his end, he spread such pestilence that he seemed almost to leave a filthier record in his death than in his life; it was as though he would extort from the guilty a punishment for his slaughter. The inhabitants being in this trouble, took the body out of the mound, beheaded it, and impaled it through the breast with a sharp stake, and herein that people found relief.

In book ii. we have the story of Aswid and Asmund. Aswid died and was buried with horse and dog. Asmund died and was buried with his friend, food being put in for him to eat. Later on the grave opened, when Asmund appeared and said: "By some strange enterprise of the power of hell the spirit of Aswid was sent up from the nether world, and with cruel tooth eats the fleet-footed (horse) and has given his dog to his abominable jaws. Not sated with devouring the horse or hound, he soon turned his swift nails upon me, tearing my cheek and taking off my ear. Hence the hideous sight of my slashed countenance, the blood spurts in the ugly wound. Yet the bringer of horrors did it not unscathed; for soon I cut off his head with my steel, and impaled his guilty carcase with a stake."

In Malaysia the vampires are mostly females, and are credited with a great fondness for fish. They are known as Langsuirs, and Skeat, in *Malay Magic*, gives the following charm for "laying" a Langsuir:—

O ye mosquito-fry at the river's mouth,

When yet a great way off ye are sharp of eye;

When near, ye are hard of heart.

When the rock in the ground opens of itself,

Then (and then only) be emboldened the hearts of my foes and opponents!

When the corpse in the ground opens of itself,

Then (and then only) be emboldened the hearts of my foes and opponents!

May your heart be softened when you behold me,

By grace of this prayer that I use, called Silam Bayn.

Abercromby, in his work on the Finns, says that the Ceremis imagine that the spirits that cause illness, especially fever and ague, are continually recruited on the death of old maids, murderers, and those that die a violent death. Whenever anyone becomes dangerously ill, the Lapps feel sure that one of his deceased relatives wants his company in the region of the dead, either from affection or to punish him for some trespass. The Truks of Altai have a similar belief. The soul after death willingly lingers for some time in the house and leaves it unwillingly, and often takes with it some other members of the family or some of the cattle.

Codrington, in his descriptive work on the Melanesians, says that there is a belief in Banks Islands in the existence of a power like that of vampires. A man or a woman would obtain this power out of a morbid desire for communion with some ghost, and in order to gain it would steal and eat a morsel of a corpse. The ghost of the dead man would then join in a close friendship with the person who had eaten, and would gratify him by afflicting anyone against whom his ghostly power might be directed. The man so afflicted would feel that something was influencing his life, and would come to dread some particular person among his neighbours, who was, therefore, suspected of being a *talamur*. This name was also given to one whose soul was supposed to go out and eat the soul or lingering life of a freshly dead corpse. There was a woman, some years ago, of whom the story is told that she made no secret of doing this, and that once on the death of a neighbour she gave notice that she should go in the night and eat the corpse. The friends of the deceased therefore kept watch in the house where the corpse lay, and at dead of night heard a scratching at the door, followed by a rustling noise close by the corpse. One of them threw a stone and seemed to hit the unknown thing; and in the morning the *talamur* was found with a bruise on her arm, which she confessed was caused by a stone thrown at her while she was eating the corpse.

Baron von Haxthausen, in his work on Transcaucasia, tells us that there once dwelt in a cavern in Armenia a vampire called Dakhanavar, who could not endure anyone to penetrate into the mountains of Ulmish Altotem or count their valleys. Everyone who attempted this had in the night his blood sucked by the monster from the soles of his feet until he died. The vampire was, however, at last outwitted by two cunning fellows. They began to count the valleys, and when night came on they lay down to sleep—taking care to place themselves with the feet of the one under the head of the other. In the night the monster came, felt as usual, and found a head; then he felt at the other end and found a head there also. "Well," cried he, "I have gone through the whole 366 valleys of these mountains, and have sucked the blood of people without end, but never yet did I come across anyone with two heads and no feet!" So saying, he ran away and was never more seen in that country, but ever after the people knew that the mountain has 366 valleys.

Even America is not free from the belief in the vampire. In one of the issues of the *Norwich* (U.S.A.) *Courier* for 1854, there is the account of an incident that occurred at Jewett, a city in that vicinity. About eight years previously, Horace Ray of Griswold had died of consumption. Afterwards, two of his children—grown-up sons—died of the same disease, the last one dying about 1852. Not long before the date of the newspaper the same fatal disease had seized another son, whereupon it was determined to exhume the bodies of the two brothers and burn them, because the dead were supposed to feed upon the living; and so long as the dead body in the grave remained undecomposed, either wholly or in part, the surviving members of the family must continue to furnish substance on which the dead body could feed. Acting under the influence of this strange superstition, the family and friends of the deceased proceeded to the burial-ground on June 8th, 1854, dug up the bodies of the deceased brothers, and burned them on the spot.

Dr Dyer, an eminent physician of Chicago, also reported in 1875 a case occurring within his own personal knowledge, where the body of a woman who had died of consumption was taken from her grave and her lungs burned, under the belief that she was drawing after her into the grave some of her surviving relatives. In 1874, according to the *Providence Journal*, in the village of Placedale, Rhode Island, Mr William Rose dug up the body of his own daughter and burned her heart, under the belief that she was wasting away the lives of other members of the family.

The vampire is not an unknown spectre in China, where the measures adopted for the riddance of the pest are generally the burning of the mortal remains of the corpse, or removing to a distance the lid of the coffin after the vampire has started on his nocturnal rounds. It is held that the air thus entering freely into the coffin will cause the contents to decay. Another Chinese cure for vampires is to watch any suspected coffin until the corpse has quitted it, and then strew rice, red peas, and bits of iron around it. The corpse, on returning, will find it impossible to pass over these things, and will thus fall an easy prey to his captors.

The following story of a Chinese vampire is related by Dr J. J. M. de Groot in his *Religious System of China* (vol. v. p. 747):—

"Liu N. N., a literary graduate of the lowest degree in Wukiang (in Kiangsu), was in charge of some pupils belonging to the Tsaing family in the Yuen-hwo district. In the season of Pure Brightness he returned home, some holidays being granted him to sweep his ancestral tombs. This duty performed, he returned to his post, and said to his wife: 'To-morrow I must go; cook some food for me at an early hour.' The woman said she would do so, and rose for the purpose at cockcrow. Their village lay on the hill behind their dwelling, facing a brook. The wife washed some rice at that brook, picked some vegetables in the garden, and had everything ready, but when it was light her husband did not rise. She went into his room to wake him up, but however often she called he gave no answer. So she opened the curtains and found him lying across the bed, headless, and not a trace of blood to be seen.

"Terror-stricken, she called the neighbours. All of them suspected her of adultery with a lover, and murder, and they warned the magistrate. This grandee came and held a preliminary inquest; he ordered the corpse to be coffined, had the woman put in fetters, and examined her; so he put her in gaol, and many months passed away without sentence being pronounced. Then a neighbour, coming uphill for some fuel, saw a neglected grave with a coffin lid bare; it was quite a sound coffin, strong and solid, and yet the lid was raised a little; so he naturally suspected that it had been opened by thieves. He summoned the people; they lifted the lid off and saw a corpse with features like a living person and a body covered with white hair. Between its arms it held the head of a man, which they recognised as that of Liu, the graduate. They reported the case to the magistrate; the coroners ordered the head to be taken away, but it was so firmly grasped in the arms of the corpse that the combined efforts of a number of men proved insufficient to draw it out. So the magistrate told them to chop off the arms of the *kiangshi* (corpse-spectre). Fresh blood gushed out of the wounds, but in Liu's head there was not a drop left, it having been sucked dry by the monster. By magisterial order the corpse was burned, and the case ended with the release of the woman from gaol."

CHAPTER X
LIVING VAMPIRES

There is, however, the living vampire, distinct and separate from the dead species. In Epirus and Thessaly there is a belief in living vampires, who leave their shepherd dwellings by night and roam about, biting and tearing men and animals and sucking their blood. In Moldavia and in Wallachia, the *murony* are real, living men who become dogs at night, with the backbone prolonged to form a sort of tail. They roam through the villages, and their main delight is to kill cattle.

In some countries the belief prevails that the soul of a living man, often of a sorcerer, leaves its proper body asleep and goes forth, perhaps in visible form of a straw or fluff of down, slips through the keyholes, and attacks its sleeping victim. If the sleeper should wake in time to clutch this tiny soul-embodiment, he may through it have his revenge by maltreating or destroying its bodily owner.

The following account was contributed by me to the *Occult Review* for July 1910. The particulars are given exactly as I wrote them down in shorthand from the narrator's dictation. My informant is a well-known medical practitioner in the West End of London, who has held various official appointments in the tropics, and I received his assurance that the incidents recorded happened exactly as they are described. Whether the Indian referred to is still alive or not is unknown, but certainly the two other principals, at the time of writing, are.

Some years ago a small number of English officials were stationed in a small place in the tropics. Their residences were about a quarter of a mile from each other, three of the bungalows standing in their own compounds and on separate elevations. Suddenly one of the officials fell ill, but the district medical officer was quite unable to trace the cause of the illness. The official in question made several applications to the Colonial Office for transfer to another station, saying he felt he should die if he remained there. At first the application was refused, but the man got worse and fell into a very depressed mental condition. He eventually wrote again, saying that if his application for transfer could not be granted he would be compelled to throw up his appointment—a serious matter for him, as he had no private means. The application was then granted; he was transferred, and he recovered his health.

About eighteen months later another official had a slight attack of fever, from which he fully recovered; but after this attack he began to complain of lassitude until he went beyond a certain distance from his residence. The moment he returned to within this distance he said he felt as though a wet blanket had been thrown over him, and nothing could rouse him from the depression which seized him. He, too, fell into a low state of health, and on his request was transferred to another station.

Shortly after this transfer the wife of the district medical officer, living within the same area, began to fail in health and became terribly depressed, apparently from no cause whatever. Previously she had been a cheerful, happy woman, indulging in games and outdoor sports of all kinds, but now she became most depressed and miserable. At last, one night, about twelve o'clock, she woke up shrieking. Her husband rushed into her room, and she said she had woken up with a most awful feeling of depression, and had seen a creature travelling along the cornice of the room. She could only describe it as having a resemblance to something between a gigantic spider and a huge jelly-fish. Her husband ascribed it to an attack of nightmare, but he was disturbed in the same manner on the following night, when his wife said she had been awake for a quarter of an hour, but had not had the strength to call him before. He found her in a state of collapse, pulse exceedingly low, temperature three degrees below normal, pallid, and in a cold sweat. He mixed her a draught which had the effect of sending her to sleep.

In the morning she said she must leave the station and go home, as to stop there would mean her death. Thinking to divert her attention, her husband took her away on a pleasure trip, when he was glad to see that she entirely recovered her former cheerful expression and high spirits. This state of things lasted until, returning home in a rickshaw alongside her husband's, her face changed and she resumed her gloomy countenance.

"There," she said, "is it not awful? I have been so well and happy all the week, and now I feel as though a pall had been thrown over me."

Matters got worse, and she became more depressed than ever, and only a few nights passed before her husband was again called to her bedside about midnight. He found his wife in a state of considerable weakness, although it was not so acute as on the previous occasion. She said to him: "I want you to examine the back of my neck and shoulders very carefully and see if there is any mark on the skin of any kind whatever."

Her husband did so, but could not find a mark.

"Get a glass and look again. See if you can find any puncture from a sharp-pointed tooth."

He made a microscopical examination, but found absolutely nothing.

"Now," said his wife, "I can tell you what is the matter. I dreamed that I was in a house where I lived when I was a girl. My little boy called out to me. I ran down to him, but when I reached the bottom of the stairs a tall, black man came towards me. I waved him off, but I could not move to get away from him, though I pushed the boy out of his reach. The man came towards me, seized me in his arms, sat down at the bottom of the stairs, put me on his knee, and proceeded to suck from a point at the upper part of the spine, just below the neck. I felt that he was drawing all the blood and life out of me. Then he threw me from him, and apparently I lost consciousness as he did so. I felt as though I was dying. Then I woke up, and I had been lying here for a quarter of an hour or twenty minutes before I was able to call you."

"Have you ever experienced anything of this character before?" asked her husband.

"No, I have not; but night after night for many months I have woken up in exactly the same state, and that has been the sole cause of my mental depression. I have not said anything about it because it seemed so foolish, but now I have had this definite dream I cannot hold my tongue any longer."

She soon passed into a peaceful sleep, and on discussing the matter the following morning with her husband she said: "I have a feeling somehow that it will not happen again. I feel quite well and strong, and all my depression is gone."

In the afternoon husband and wife were going together to the club, when around the corner of the jungle came a tall Indian, the owner of a large number of milch cattle, and reputed to be a wealthy man. The surgeon's wife suddenly stopped, turned pale, and said immediately: "That is the man I saw in my dream."

The husband went directly up to the man and said to him: "Look here, I will give you twelve hours to get out of this place. I know everything that happened last night at midnight, and I will kill you like a dog if I find you here in twelve hours' time."

The Indian disappeared the same night, taking with him only a few valuables and a little loose money. He left behind him the money that was deposited in the bank, as well as the whole of his property. His forty head of cattle, worth eighty dollars each, were impounded, and no news had been heard of him five years afterwards. Since his departure no one has complained of depression and lassitude in that area.

CHAPTER XI
THE VAMPIRE IN LITERATURE

The subject of vampirism does not appear to have attracted litterateurs greatly. True, there are the operas of Palma, Hart, Marschner, and von Lindpainter; and Philostratus and Phlegon of Tralles have discoursed upon the phenomena. There are not, however, many works of fiction based upon the topic, or many poems in which the subject is introduced. There is an Anglo-Saxon poem with the title *A Vampyre of the Fens*, and a long, wearisome novel, full of gruesome details, entitled *Varney the Vampire*. Among modern authors, Mr Bram Stoker has made the vampire the foundation of his exciting romance *Dracula*; but mention of these works almost exhausts the references to separate works upon the subject.

Nor are the references to vampires and vampirism in the ancient Greek authors more numerous. The phantom of Achilles is represented by Euripides (*Hec.*, 109, 599) as appearing on his tomb clad in golden armour and appeased by the sacrifice of a young virgin, whose blood he drank. Œdipus also in Sophocles (*Œd. Col.*, 621), when foretelling a defeat which the Thebans would sustain near his tomb, declares that his cold, dead body will drink their warm blood. Human victims were offered at the funeral pyre of Patroclus in the *Iliad* (vol. i.).

Though human beings are not sacrificed in the *Odyssey*, yet the blood of slaughtered sheep was eagerly lapped up by the ghosts consulted by Odysseus (xi. 45, 48, 95, 96, 153, etc.). A sheep was also to be sacrificed at the tombs of mortals, and its blood was supposed to be an offering acceptable to the departed spirit.

Pausanias, Strabo, Ælian, and Suidas relate the legend of Ulysses in his wanderings coming to the town of Temesa, in Italy, where one of his associates was stoned to death by the townsmen for having ravished a virgin. His ghost forthwith haunted the inhabitants, and caused them such annoyance that many were thinking seriously of leaving the town when they were told by Apollo's oracle that to appease him they must build the hero a temple, and sacrifice to him yearly the most beautiful virgin they had among them. The temple was accordingly raised: access to the sacred enclosure was prohibited to all except the priests, on penalty of death. An engraving of the evil spirit that is alleged to have infested Temesa is given on page 18 of Beaumont's *Treatise on Spirits* (ed. 1705).

Philostratus, in his *Life of Apollonius of Tyana* (iv. 25, p. 165), says that the long intercourse which took place between a female spectre and the Corinthian Menippus was but a prelude to the feast of flesh and blood in which she meant to revel after their marriage.

Some have described the Hebrew *lilith* as a vampire, but the *Jewish Encyclopædia* states that: "There is nothing in the Talmud to indicate that the *lilith* was a vampire." She was regarded as a nocturnal demon, flying about in the form of a night-owl, and stealing children, and was held to have permission to kill all children sinfully begotten, even from a lawful wife. The *lilith* is held to have the same signification as the Greek *strix* and *lamiæ*, who were sorceresses or magicians, seeking to put to death new-born children. The ancient Greeks believed that these *lamiæ* devoured children, or sucked away all their blood until they died. Euripides and the scholiast of Aristophanes mention the *lilith* as a dangerous monster, the enemy of mortals; and Ovid describes the *strigæ* as dangerous birds, which fly by night and seek for infants to devour them and nourish themselves with their blood. The *aluka* of Proverbs xxx. 15 is more akin to the vampire. It is a blood-sucking, insatiable monster; the word is synonymous with *algul*, the well-known demon of the Arabian popular stories, "the man-devouring demon of the waste," known as the ghoul or goule in the translated edition of the *Arabian Nights*.

Goethe, in his ballad *The Bride of Corinth*, describes how a young Athenian visits a friend of his father, to whose daughter he had been betrothed, and is disturbed at midnight by the appearance of the vampire spectre of her whom death has prevented from becoming his bride, and who, when detected, says:—

> From my grave to wander I am forc'd,
>
> Still to seek The Good's long-sever'd link,
>
> Still to love the bridegroom I have lost,
>
> And the life-blood of his heart to drink;
>
> When his race is run,
>
> I must hasten on,
>
> And the young must 'neath my vengeance sink.

There is one scant reference to the subject in Shelley's poems. Byron, in his poem *The Giaour*, has the following passage:—

> But first on earth as vampire sent
>
> Thy corse shall from its tomb be rent:
>
> Then ghastly haunt thy native place,
>
> And suck the blood of all thy race.

Dryden relates:—

> Lo, in my walks where wicked elves have been,
>
> The learning of the parish now is seen—
>
> From fiends and imps he sets the village free,
>
> There haunts not any incubus but he:
>
> The maids and women need no danger fear
>
> To walk by night and sanctity so near.

Scott, in *Rokeby*, has the following lines:—

> For like the bat of Indian brakes,
>
> Her pinions fan the wound she makes,
>
> And soothing thus the dreamer's pains,
>
> She drinks the life-blood from the veins.

The following legend is related in vol. ii. of *Minstrelsy of the Scottish Border*, and is referred to in a footnote to Southey's *Thalaba the Destroyer* (p. 108, ed. 1814):—

In the year 1058 a young man of noble birth had been married in Rome, and during the period of his nuptial feast, having gone with his companions to play at ball, he put his marriage ring on the finger of a broken statue of Venus in the area, to remain while he was engaged in recreation. Desisting from the exercise, he found the finger on which he had put his ring contracted firmly against the palm, and attempted in vain either to break or disengage the ring. He concealed the circumstances from his companions, and returned at night with a servant, when he found the finger extended and the ring gone. He dissembled the loss and returned to his wife; but when he attempted to embrace her he found himself prevented by something dark and dense, which was tangible if not visible, interposing between them; and he heard a voice saying: "Embrace me! for I am Venus, whom this day you wedded, and I will not restore your ring." As this was constantly repeated, he consulted his relatives, who had recourse to Palumbus, the priest, skilled in necromancy. He directed the young man to go at a certain hour of the night to a spot among the ruins of ancient Rome where four roads meet, and wait silently till he saw a company pass by, and then, without uttering a word, to deliver a letter which he gave him to a majestic being who rode in a chariot after the rest of the company. The young man did as he was directed, and saw the company of all ages, classes and ranks, on horse and on foot, some joyful and others sad, pass along; among whom he distinguished a woman in a meretricious dress, who, from the tenuity of her garments, seemed almost naked. She rode on a mule; her long hair, which flowed over her shoulders, was bound with a golden fillet; and in her hand was a golden rod with which she directed her mule. In the close of the procession a tall, majestic figure appeared in a chariot adorned with emeralds and pearls, who fiercely asked the young man what he did there. He presented the letter in silence, which the demon dared not refuse. As soon as he had read, lifting up his hands to heaven, he exclaimed: "Almighty God! how long wilt Thou endure the iniquities of the sorcerer Palumbus!" and immediately despatched some of his attendants, who, with much difficulty, extorted the ring from Venus and restored it to its owner, whose infernal banns were thus dissolved. This legend was made the foundation of Liddell's poem, *The Vampire Bride*.

Dion Boucicault wrote and produced a vampire play entitled *The Phantom*, the scene of which was laid in the ruins of Raby Castle. Anyone remaining in these ruins for one night met with certain death before the morning. The only sign of violence to be found was a wound on the right side of the throat, but no blood was to be seen. The face of the victim was white and the gaze fixed, as though the person had died from fright.

In April 1819 a story entitled "The Vampyre" appeared in *Colburn's New Monthly Magazine*, which was attributed to Lord Byron, but which was really from the pen of Dr John William Polidori (uncle of William Michael Rossetti), who was for a time Lord Byron's travelling physician. The work was also published separately, but the authorship was denied by Lord Byron. Polidori immediately claimed responsibility for the work, and the correspondence and statement of facts published in Rossetti's *Diary of Doctor John William Polydori* show how the mistake occurred.

The following poem appears in the *Life of James Clerk Maxwell*, by Lewis Campbell and William Garnett, and was written by Maxwell in 1845, when he was fourteen years of age:—

THE VAMPYRE

COMPYLT INTO MEETER BY JAMES CLERK MAXWELL

Thair is a knichte rydis through the wood,

And a douchty knichte is hee.

And sure hee is on a message sent,

He rydis sae hastilie.

Hee passit the aik, and hee passit the birk,

And hee passit monie a tre,

Bot plesant to him was the saugh sae slim,

For beneath it hee did see

The boniest ladye that ever hee saw,

Scho was sae schyn and fair.

And thair scho sat, beneath the saugh,

Kaiming hir gowden hair.

And then the knichte—"Oh ladye brichte,

What chance has broucht you here?

But say the word, and ye schall gang

Back to your kindred dear."

Then up and spok the ladye fair—

"I have nae friends or kin,

Bot in a little boat I live,

Amidst the waves' loud din."

Then answered thus the douchty knichte—

"I'll follow you through all,

For gin ye bee in a littel boat,

The world to it seemis small."

They goed through the wood, and through the wood,

To the end of the wood they came:

And when they came to the end of the wood

They saw the salt sea faem.

And then they saw the wee, wee boat,

That daunced on the top of the wave,

And first got in the ladye fair,

And then the knichte sae brave.

They got into the wee, wee boat,

And rowed wi' a' their micht;

When the knichte sae brave, he turnit about,

And lookit at the ladye bricht;

He lookit at her bonnie cheik,

And hee lookit at hir twa bricht eyne,

Bot hir rosie cheik growe ghaistly pale,

And schoe seymit as scho deid had been.

The fause, fause knichte growe pale wi' frichte,

And his hair rose up on end,

For gane-by days cam to his mynde,

And his former luve he kenned.

Then spake the ladye—"Thou, fause knichte,

Hast done to me much ill,

Thou didst forsake me long ago,

Bot I am constant still;

For though I ligg in the woods sae cald,

At rest I canna bee

Until I sucks the gude lyfe blude

Of the man that gart me dee."

Hee saw hir lipps were wet wi' blude,

And hee saw hir lufelesse eyne,

And loud hee cry'd, "Get frae my syde,

Thou vampyr corps encleane!"

Bot no, hee is in hir magic boat,

And on the wyde, wyde sea;

And the vampyr suckis his gude lyfe blude,

Sho suckis hym till hee dee.

So now beware, whoe'er you are,

That walkis in this lone wood:

Beware of that deceitfull spright,

The ghaist that suckis the blude.

Mr Reginald Hodder, in *The Vampire* (William Rider & Son, Ltd.), has developed a theory which is a novel one in the annals of vampirism. The principal character is a living woman, a member of a secret sisterhood, who is forced to exercise her powers as a vampire to prevent loss of vitality. This power, however, is exercised through the medium of a metallic talisman, and the main thread of the story turns on the struggle for the possession of this talisman. It is wrested ultimately from the hands of those who would use it for malignant purposes, but its recovery is only accomplished by means of a number of extraordinary—though who would dare say impossible?—occult phenomena.

CHAPTER XII
FACT OR FICTION?

While some writers, belonging mainly to what is popularly known as the orthodox school of theology or professing a materialistic philosophy, have expressed an entire disbelief in the alleged phenomena, others, on the other hand, accepting generally the spiritistic or spiritualistic philosophy, have admitted the possibility of the phenomena, though not pledging their acceptance of all or any of the many stories told concerning the deeds, or rather the misdeeds, of the apparitions.

Dr Pierart, the well-known French *savant*, maintained that "the facts of vampirism are as well attested by inquiries made as are the facts of catalepsy," and that "the facts of vampirism are as old as the world," and pointed to the fact that Tertullian and St Augustine spoke of them.

Gabriele D'Annunzio was another firm believer in their existence. In his *Triumph of Death*, translated by Georgina Harding, we read: "What have they not done? Candia told of all the different means they had tried, all the exorcisms they had resorted to. The priest had come and, after covering the child's head with the end of his stole, had repeated verses from the Gospel. The mother had hung up a wax cross, blessed on Ascension Day, over a door, and had sprinkled the hinges with holy water and repeated the Creed three times in a loud voice; she had tied up a handful of salt in a piece of linen and hung it round the neck of her dying child. The father had 'done the seven nights'—that is, for seven nights he had waited in the dark behind a lighted lantern, attentive to the slightest sound, ready to catch and grapple with the vampire. A single prick with the pin sufficed to make her visible to the human eye. But the seven nights' watch had been fruitless, for the child wasted away and grew more hopelessly feeble from hour to hour. At last, in despair, the father had consulted with a wizard, by whose advice he had called a dog and put the body behind the door. The vampire could not then enter the house till she counted every hair on its body."

Calmet's explanation of the spectres so much talked of in Hungary, Moravia, Poland, and elsewhere is that they are nothing but persons that are still alive in their graves, though without motion or respiration; and that the freshness and ruddy colour of their blood, the flexibility of their limbs, and their crying out when their hearts were run through with a stick, or their heads cut off, were demonstrative proofs of their being still alive. "But this," he says, "does not affect the principal difficulty at which I stick, namely, how they come out of and go into their graves, without leaving any mark of the earth's being removed; and how they appear to carry former clothes. If they are not really dead, why do they return to their graves again and not stay in the land of the living? Why do they suck the blood of their relations, and torment and pester persons that should naturally be true to them and never give them any offence? On the other hand, if it be nothing but a mere whim of the persons infested, whence comes it that these carcases are found in their graves uncorrupted, full of blood, with their limbs pliant and flexible, and their feet dirty, the next day after they have been patrolling about and frightening the neighbourhood, whilst nothing of this sort can be discovered in other carcases that were buried at the same time and in the same mound? Whence is it that they come no more after they are burned or impaled?"

Other writers have accepted the theory that the subjects are not really dead, but are only in a death-like condition. The Germans express this condition of apparent death and of the perfect preservation of the living body by the term *scheintod*, which is, perhaps, better than the English term "suspended animation." Dr Herbert Mayo describes the special condition of vampires as a "death-trance"—a positive status, a period of repose, the duration of which is sometimes definite and predetermined, though unknown, and says that the patient sometimes awakes suddenly when the term of the death-trance has expired. During this trance-period the action of the heart, breathing, voluntary motion, as well as feeling and intelligence and the vegetable changes in the body, are said to be suspended. Two instances of the death-trance are quoted.

Cardinal Espinosa, prime minister under Philip the Second of Spain, died, as it was supposed, after a short illness. His rank entitled him to be embalmed. Accordingly, the body was opened for that purpose. The lungs and heart had just been brought into view, when the latter was seen to beat. The cardinal, awakening at the fatal moment, had still strength enough left to seize with his hand the knife of the anatomist.

On the 23rd of September 1763, the Abbé Prévost, the French novelist and compiler of travels, was seized with a fit in the forest of Chantilly. The body was found and conveyed to the residence of the nearest clergyman. It was supposed that death had taken place through apoplexy. But the local authorities, desiring to be satisfied of the fact, ordered the body to be examined. During the process the poor Abbé uttered a cry of agony. It was too late.

Among Theosophists and Continental spiritists a solution to the problem is found in their teaching concerning the astral body and the astral plane, as conveyed by Madame Blavatsky in *Isis Unveiled*.

It is held that so long as the astral form is not entirely separated from the body there is a liability that it may be forced by magnetic attraction to re-enter it. Sometimes it will be only half-way out when the corpse, which presents the appearance of death, is buried. In such cases the astral body voluntarily re-enters the mortal frame, and then one of two things happens—either the unhappy victim will writhe in the agonising torture of suffocation, or if he has been grossly material he becomes a vampire. It is held that this ethereal form can go wherever it pleases, and that it is possible for this astral body to feed on human victims and carry the sustenance to the corpus lying within the tomb by means of an invisible cord of connection, the nature of which is at present unknown; but psychical researchers—and these number many eminent scientists—have of late years devoted their efforts towards the elucidation of the phenomenon known as the projection of the double; and this, if scientifically and satisfactorily explained, will give the clue to many of the phenomena of vampirism.

This "double" may sometimes during life be projected unconsciously, and sometimes purposely, by means of hypnotism or provoked somnambulism. An example of the former appeared in the *Journal du Magnétisme* for October 1909, and the translation of the account was published in the *Annals of Psychical Science* for January-March 1910, and is here reproduced. The narrator is M. Antonio Salazar of Mexico.

"A Romantic Case of Projection of the Double

"In 1889 I lived at Juatlahuaca, in the state of Oaxaca, Mexico. For a long time I passionately loved the woman who afterwards became my wife.

"At the beginning of 1890, through one of those unfortunate disagreements which occasionally arise between parents and their children, those of my beloved one, wishing to put an end to our mutual love, separated us by taking her to the mountains; but this only increased our love, because of the difficulties and our desire to see each other.

"Several months passed after our separation, and though the distance between us was not great, we had to take into account the vigilance with which she was surrounded, and which was a greater obstacle than the difficulties of the road.

"One night, when I was feeling, as usual, very sad and gloomy, the thought came to me to say to my servant: 'Jeanette, if any morning you come into my room and do not find me, do not look for me; take the keys and open the shop. If at midday I have not arrived, you can seek for me in the mountains.'

"'Ah, sir,' she replied, 'I would never oppose myself to your commands, if what you tell me did not concern persons whom I love and respect, because you will never thereby accomplish your object.'

"I knew that she was right, and I thought that the best thing I could do was to go to sleep and try to calm my imagination. She also retired, much distressed, and imploring all the saints, to whom she prayed, to prevent any unfortunate incident which would threaten the lives of three persons—my *fiancée*, her father, and myself.

"The following day I awoke with the same project in my mind, but before carrying it out I wished to inform my *fiancée* as to the day and hour at which I hoped to speak to her. She replied by showing me the rashness of my project, and offering to do all she could to overcome the obstacles which prevented her from returning to live in the town, which she hoped to do in a few days, and which came to pass as she had predicted. I reckoned, however, on my sagacity and youthful ardour to realise my project before my *fiancée* was able to return.

"One day, when my mind was indulging itself in all kinds of fancies, I thought it would be quite easy to elude the vigilance of all those who were around my *fiancée*, and who were opposed to our meeting. When night came on I continued to think of my project, and I resolved to lie down and try to sleep.

"I passed a very disturbed night, waking frequently, and when the day began to break, the servant came to my room to bid me 'good morning,' and to ask for the keys of the shop.

"'How have you passed the night, sir?' she asked.

"'Rather badly, Jeanette. I have dreamed continually, and it is impossible for me to give you an idea of all the dangers and precipices which I thought I overcame and crossed; it seems to me that I went over the mountain road which leads to the farm, but it was a very different road. I dreamed that our interview was prevented, I do not know how, and that I had a long walk home again. What can it all mean?'

"'It is only the result of your wishes and preoccupation in regard to the young lady. She will soon return, and then these follies will disappear.'

"I very soon forgot all about what I have just described, and so did my servant, for neither of us attached any importance to a dream; but, after a short time, a messenger from the farm handed me a letter, in which my *fiancée* reproached me for my violence, my bad conduct and disobedience in going there in defiance of the commands and wishes of her father.

"'What? I? No. Never! Tell your mistress that, although I have thought of going to see her, I have never carried out my desires; if I have not done so, it has not been through lack of courage and will on my part, but only because of my desire to please her and not to oppose her wishes.'

"'But we saw you.'

"'Me?'

"'Yes, sir—you.'

"'You are telling an untruth. I have not been out. My servant can corroborate that; and, further, I have nothing to lose by telling the truth.'

"'That may be as you please, but it is true that you spoke to me; you questioned me on the subject of Mademoiselle—desired me to tell her that you were there and wished to speak to her.'

"'These are illusions on your part; you have been dreaming.'

"'That is possible; but there were two, three, all the servants, who also saw you. You did not arrive until nearly midnight; you were dressed as you are now, and riding a white horse, which you fastened to the gnarled oak. We could all recognise you by the moonlight, and you were going towards the side door when I stopped you from entering.

"'Hearing our voices, the dogs began to bark, which caused all the servants to get up. You were recognised by my master and the young lady, who fell on her knees before her father, beseeching him not to fire on you. Without showing any fear, you returned step by step to your horse and went down the mountain again. My master was much annoyed with you, called his confidential servant Marino, ordered him to follow you and not to be afraid, but to fire on you two or three times, as he would be responsible. Marino set out, and, although he walked quickly and tried all he could to catch you up, he could not do so. A curious phenomenon aroused his attention, which was that he always saw you going at the same pace, and he had not the courage to fire his rifle.

"'You arrived at the entrance to the town about five o'clock in the morning; the moon was setting and the day commencing to break. Before you arrived at the first crossing of the streets you began to run, and turned quickly along the first street in the town; and though Marino ran after you, he lost sight of you at the next crossing.'

"My persecutor, frightened by what he had seen, returned immediately to the farm to inform his master of what had taken place, and which seemed very extraordinary and supernormal.

"For a long time this adventure, of which I was the unconscious hero, made a great stir in the town."

Colonel de Rochas, a distinguished French savant, has made this question of the externalisation or projection of the double and of the motricity and sensibility of the subject his special and patient study, and has embodied the results of many of his experiments in separate works. Some have also been published in the pages of the *Annals of Psychical Science*, so that the reader who is particularly interested in the question will have no difficulty in finding material for further consideration and study.

The Société Magnétique de France has also conducted extensive experiments in this field of research, particulars of which are published from time to time in the *Journal du Magnétisme*. The following theoretical explanation given at the conclusion of the report of a series of these experiments is reprinted from the *Annals* for July-September 1910:—

"We know that the phantom is the psychical body projected from the physical body. It is that which enjoys or suffers, thinks, wishes, judges, and perceives all sensations. It is constantly animated by extremely rapid vibratory movements which are certainly the same as when it is within the body. This principle being admitted, we understand that, when it animates the body, its vibratory movements are not projected outside, and that it exercises no appreciable action on other organisms in its neighbourhood. But when it is outside the body its movements are easily externalised. Then the phantom and another person, vibrating in unison, represent two stringed instruments which sound at the same time when one only is touched. If I can obtain this transmission at great distances, we can explain this strange and unexpected phenomenon by the theory of wireless telegraphy or telephony."

The results of the many experiments conducted by and under the auspices of French scientists in particular tend to indicate that in the near future an explanation of the phenomena of vampirism will be forthcoming.

BIBLIOGRAPHY

Abercromby's *Finns.*

Leo Allatius.

Barth's *The Religions of India.*

Bartholin's *de Causa contemptûs mortis.*

Beaumont's *Treatise on Spirits.*

Blavatsky's *Isis Unveiled.*

Calmet's *Dissertation upon Apparitions.*

Calmet's *The Phantom World.*

Hugh Clifford's *In Court and Kampong.*

Codrington's *Melanesians.*

Conway's *Demonology and Folk-lore.*

William Crooke's *Popular Religion and Folk-lore of Northern India.*

Gabriele D'Annunzio's *The Triumph of Death.*

De Schartz, *Magia Postuma.*

C. M. Doughty's *Arabia Deserta.*

Eaves' *Modern Vampirism.*

Encyclopædia Britannica.

Eyre's *Discoveries in Central Australia.*

Farrer's *Primitive Manners and Customs.*

Fornari's *History of Sorcerers.*

Fortis' *Travels into Dalmatia.*

Frazer's *Golden Bough.*

Goethe's *Bride of Corinth.*

Baring Gould's *Book of Were Wolves.*

Grimm's *Teutonic Mythology.*

J. J. Morgan de Groot's *Religious System of China.*

Baron von Haxthausen's *Transcaucasia.*

Hikayat Abdullah.

Reginald Hodder's *The Vampire.*

Jewish Encyclopædia.

Keightley's *Fairy Mythology.*

T. S. Knowlson's *Origin of Popular Superstitions.*

Leake's *Travels in Northern Greece.*

Liddell's *The Vampire Bride.*

Mackenzie and Irby's *Travels in the Slavonic Provinces of Turkey in Europe.*

Mayo's *On the Truths contained in Popular Superstitions.*

Minstrelsy of the Scottish Border (vol. ii.).

More's *Antidote against Atheism.*

Nider's *Formicarius.*

Laurence Oliphant's *Scientific Religion.*

Pashley's *Crete* (vol. ii.).

Polidori's *The Vampyre.*

Michael Psellus' *Dialogus de Operationibus Dæmonum.*

Ralston's *Russian Folk Tales.*

Ralston's *Songs of the Russian People.*

Roussel's *Transfusion of Human Blood.*

Rycaut's *The Present State of the Greek and Armenian Churches.*

Rymer's *Varney the Vampire.*

St Clair and Brophy's *Bulgaria.*

Saxo Grammaticus' *Danish History.*

Sayce's *Ancient Empires of the East.*

Scoffern's *Stray Leaves of Science and Folk-lore.*

Sir Walter Scott's translation of *Eyrbyggia Saga.*

Siegbert's *Chronicle.*

W. W. Skeat's *Malay Magic.*

Skeat and Blagden's *Pagan Races of the Malay Peninsula.*

Southey's *Thalaba the Destroyer.*

Bram Stoker's *Dracula.*

R. Campbell Thompson's *The Devils and Evil Spirits of Babylonia.*

J. Pitton de Tournefort's *A Voyage into the Levant.*

Tozer's *Researches in the Highlands of Turkey.*

Trumbull's *Blood Covenant.*

Turner's *Nineteen Years in Polynesia.*

Tylor's *Primitive Culture.*

Voltaire's *Dictionnaire Philosophique.*

Horace Walpole's *Reminiscences.*

Westermarck's *Origin and Development of Moral Ideas.*

William of Newbury.

PERIODICAL LITERATURE

All the Year Round (vol. xxv.).

Annals of Psychical Science.

Blackwood's Magazine (vol. lxi.).

Borderland.

Chambers's Journal (vol. lxxiii.).

Colburn's Magazine (vol. vii.).

Contemporary Review (July 1885).

Gentleman's Magazine (July 1851).

Household Words (vol. xi.).

Journal du Magnétisme.

Journal Indian Archipelago (vol. i.).

Lippincott's Magazine (vol. xlvii.).

London Journal (March 1732).

New Monthly Magazine (1st April 1819).

Nineteenth Century (September 1885).

Notes and Queries.

Occult Review.

Open Court (vol. vii.).

Revue Spiritualiste (vol. iv.).

St James's Magazine (vol. x.).

Wonderful Magazine (1764).